A CENTURY OF
WHISKY

Testing the strength of whisky in William Grant & Sons' Glasgow warehouse, *c.* 1937.

A CENTURY OF
WHISKY

GAVIN SMITH

WHSmith

First published in the United Kingdom in 2001 by
Sutton Publishing Limited exclusively for
WHSmith, Greenbridge Road, Swindon SN3 3LD

Copyright © Gavin Smith, 2001

British Library Cataloguing in Publication Data
A catalogue record for this book is available from the British Library.

ISBN 0-7509-2847-6

Illustrations

Front endpaper: Pulteney distillery warehouse.
Back endpaper: Talisker distillery, Carbost, Isle of Skye.
Half title page: Fettercairn distillery, Angus, 1990s.
Title page: HRH Prince Charles sampling a dram of Laphroaig during a visit to the distillery in 1994, marking the award of a Royal Warrant to the Islay single malt. The British royal family has long taken an interest in the Scotch whisky industry, with King George IV reputedly only drinking illicitly distilled Glenlivet, while Queen Victoria was once observed by Prime Minister Gladstone adding whisky to her glass of claret!

Typeset in 11/14pt Photina and produced by Sutton Publishing Limited, Phoenix Mill, Thrupp, Stroud, Gloucestershire GL5 2BU. Printed and bound in England by J.H. Haynes & Co. Ltd, Sparkford.

Spirit vat, The Glenlivet distillery, 1930s.

Contents

Whyte & Mackay 'empties' being removed from 10 Downing Street during Harold Wilson's 1964–70 administration. When Prime Minister Sir Winston Churchill noted in a 1945 minute to the Ministry of Food 'On no account reduce the barley for whisky. This takes years to mature and is an invaluable export and dollar producer. Having regard to all our other difficulties about exports, it would be most improvident not to preserve this characteristic British element of ascendancy.' As Prime Minister, Margaret Thatcher was known to enjoy her dram, and Orkney-born Chancellor of the Exchequer Norman Lamont favoured Highland Park as his Budget Speech tipple.

Introduction

The recorded history of Scotch whisky dates back to 1494, yet it is really only during the last century or so that 'Scotch' has truly become a drink for the world. From its cottage industry origins, Scotch whisky has developed into big business. Domestic consumption remains gratifyingly high, but around 90 per cent of Scotch whisky sales are made abroad and, according to the Scotch Whisky Association, thirty-one bottles of Scotch are exported every second. Exports are worth in excess of £2 billion per year, and in total some 75 million nine-litre cases are sold annually. It is interesting to note that more Scotch is sold in France in one month than Cognac in an entire year!

Scotch whisky retails in more than 200 countries around the world, and is one of Britain's top five export-earners. The industry provides 11,200 jobs, often in economically fragile areas, and supports a further 30,000 positions with suppliers and support services. In effect, whisky plays a part in one in every fifty-four Scottish jobs. Apart from its obvious financial significance, the spirit is also one of the defining icons of 'Scottishness' in the popular consciousness, and has an important role in Scottish tourism.

All of this seems a long way from the first surviving piece of documented history relating to Scotch whisky, which takes the form of a reference in the 1494 Exchequer Rolls for '. . . eight bolls of malt to Friar John Cor wherewith to make aquaviate'. Cor was a Benedictine monk at Lindores Abbey in Fife, and aquavitae is Latin for 'water of life', equivalent to the Gaelic *uisge beatha*, ultimately anglicised to 'whisky'.

Distillation had almost certainly been taking place in Scotland for many years prior to its mention in the Exchequer Rolls, and discovery of the art is usually credited to the Ancient Egyptians. Irish monks were making spirit by the late twelfth century for medicinal purposes, and it is likely that the secrets of distillation travelled to the Hebridean islands and the western Scottish mainland from Ireland. Eleven years after Friar Cor received his bolls of malt, Edinburgh's Guild of Surgeon

A distillery worker samples the spirit produced from the replica 500-year-old pot still developed at Invergordon grain distillery, Easter Ross, 1994.

Barbers was granted a monopoly on whisky production in the Scottish capital, highlighting the continuing medicinal significance of the spirit.

Until the eighteenth century, most Scottish distilling operations were small in scale and rural in location, usually fitting neatly into the agricultural calendar. Whisky-making provided an attractive way of converting surplus barley into a higher value 'currency', and many tenants paid their rent in liquid form. In addition to barley, the production of whisky required pure water and peat for fuel, and most areas with ready access to malting barley would almost certainly have plentiful supplies of the other two principal necessities near at hand.

In 1644 the first excise duty was imposed on spirits in Scotland, and for the best part of the next two centuries many Scottish distillers would go to great trouble to hide their stills and distribute their 'make' outwith the law. Pitted against the wily smugglers with their intimate knowledge of the local terrain and the support of a majority of the populace were the hapless 'gaugers' or excise officers, who faced an almost impossible task in trying to curb the growth of illicit distillation.

The original oil sketch for *An illicit whisky still in the Highlands*, by Sir Edwin Landseer (1802–73), in the possession of William Grant & Sons.

During the mid-eighteenth century, large-scale legal distilleries began to be developed in the Scottish Lowlands, encouraged by various pieces of government legislation designed to stimulate the legal trade and suppress illicit whisky-making. The important Wash Act of 1784 reduced the level of duty paid by distillers and introduced the theoretical 'Highland Line' which separated distilleries of the Highlands from those of the Lowlands, and ran from the Firth of Clyde in the west to the Firth of Tay in the east. The level of duty paid by small-scale distillers north of the line was lower than it was in the Lowlands in an attempt to encourage legal Highland distilling.

In 1816 the Small Stills Act was passed, abolishing the different levels of duty in Highlands and Lowlands, as by this time a thriving trade in whisky smuggled from the Highlands into the Lowlands had developed. This was partly because the Highland whisky was cheaper, but also because it was usually of higher quality than that produced in the Lowlands.

The Small Stills Act also lowered the minimum legal capacity of stills to 40 gallons, in yet another attempt to persuade the Highland distillers that it really was better to operate inside the law rather than outwith it. This did cause the creation of forty-five new distilleries in the Highlands, to add to the existing dozen, but illicit distillation continued to be a problem until the 1823 Excise Act – the most far-reaching piece of excise legislation ever enacted in Britain. It is no exaggeration to say that this Act allowed the development of large-scale legal whisky distilling, and led to the powerful and successful industry we have today.

The Act of 1823 reduced duty by a significant amount in order to encourage legal distilling, and the legislation was notably successful, with the amount of legally distilled whisky rising from 2 million gallons in 1823 to 6 million gallons just two years later. In the same period, the number of distilleries operating in Scotland doubled. With the support of key Scottish landowners such as the Duke of Gordon, illicit distilling fell as dramatically as the amount of legally distilled spirit rose in the years following the passing of the Excise Act.

Along with this Excise Act, a key factor in the growth of whisky as an important and international drink was the development of the Coffey or 'patent' still that produced grain whisky. The man who started the grain spirit revolution was Robert Stein, a member of a famous Lowland distilling dynasty, who in 1827 pioneered the construction of a revolutionary new kind of still that worked on a continuous rather than a 'batch' basis in the manner of the established pot still.

Stein's early work was refined by a former Inspector-General of Excise in Ireland, Aeneas Coffey, who patented his eponymous still design in 1831. Coffey or 'patent' stills could produce far greater quantities of spirit than their pot still counterparts, and utilised comparatively cheap grains such as maize, though the make was quite bland, and much of it was rectified into gin in England, rather than consumed in its original form.

Unofficially, grain spirit was sometimes added to pot still whisky by publicans to increase their profit margins, but Andrew Usher of Edinburgh was the first person to begin experimenting with combinations of whiskies of different ages, and can justifiably be credited as the founding father of blended whisky. His contribution is often overshadowed by that of high-profile figures such as the charismatic Tommy Dewar and

An 1887 advertisement for a Coffey still.

James Buchanan, who were to become the public face of the blended whisky industry.

Usher was the Edinburgh agent for the Glenlivet distillery, and in 1853 – when the 'vatting' of whiskies of varying ages from one distillery became legal for the first time – he began to market a highly regarded vatting of Glenlivets under the name Usher's OVG (Old Vatted Glenlivet). Usher's aim was to produce a drink with the consistency necessary to satisfy major markets outwith Scotland, but with the passing of the Spirits Act of 1860 he was able to make significant advances on his pioneering work. The Spirits Act increased duty substantially, but also made it legal for the first time to blend whiskies from different distilleries before duty was paid.

It was a logical step for Usher to cut the cost of his whiskies by mixing cheaper grain whisky with a variety of malts. Not only was the cost reduced, but the resultant drink gained a smoothness from the grain, and lacked the ferocity and inconsistency that kept malt whiskies out of the drawing rooms of polite society.

During the late 1870s Perth whisky blender Arthur Bell wrote 'Several fine whiskies blended together please the palates of a greater number of people, than one whisky unmixed, consequently I have long adopted the practice. . .'.

The development of blended whisky and the astonishing surge of entrepreneurial activity that accompanied its development from the final quarter of the nineteenth century onwards meant that a greater number of palates came to be pleased than anyone involved could ever have imagined. Whisky was to become a drink for the world.

Making Whisky &
the Art of Blending

Idiosyncratic stills at Pulteney distillery, Wick, 1990s. The wash still in the foreground has a remarkably large 'boiling ball' for its size, which adds to the comparative lightness of the finished whisky without detracting from its character.

The process of producing malt whisky has, in essence, changed little through the centuries, and still owes much to the skills of the individuals charged with making it. One of the great joys of malt whiskies is their individuality, and the make of no two distilleries is ever the same. While it is possible to copy production equipment and methods, use the same water source, barley, and yeasts, and mature for the same duration in the same kind of casks within the same microclimate, the result will always be two distinctly different spirits. An enormous amount of money has been invested in the search for a definitive scientific evaluation of the variables in malt whisky making, but an element of mystery remains.

The business of making malt whisky begins by malting barley in order to induce germination. In a traditional maltings, the barley is steeped in water for two or three days, then spread on a malting floor, where rootlets develop as germination begins.

So that the malt retains the sugars essential for fermentation, the partially germinated 'green malt' as it is known is transferred to a kiln after about seven days and dried over a fire or by jets of hot air, with peat used to impart flavour. The amount of peat used during kilning has a major influence on the character of the finished whisky.

Once dried, the malt is ground in a mill to produce 'grist', after which the process of mashing begins. The grist is mixed with hot water in large mash tuns to extract fermentable sugars, and the sweet liquid that results from mashing is known as 'wort'. What is left behind is called 'draff', and as it is high in protein it makes excellent cattle feed.

The wort is pumped from the mash tuns into large washbacks, where yeast is added in order to promote fermentation, and create alcohol. The end product of fermentation is a liquor known as 'wash', and at this point distillation begins. So far, the processes of whisky-making have been similar to those used to brew beer, but now the wash is transferred into copper wash stills, where it is brought to the boil. Alcohol boils at a lower temperature than water, so the alcohol vapours rise from the still first, and are condensed into liquid when they pass through pipes in tanks filled with cold water.

The alcohol produced needs to be re-distilled in order to obtain the pure spirit that will mature into whisky, and this takes place in smaller vessels, known as spirit stills. The heating process is repeated, but this time the early distillation, called foreshots, is too strong and impure to be used, and is piped into a low wines charger to be re-distilled later. The last flow from the still is the feints, which is too weak and impure to be used in its existing form, and it too is later re-distilled.

The spirit that comes from the stills is known as 'new make'. It is a clear liquid, and before it is poured into oak casks to mature it is reduced from its natural strength down to around 63–64 per cent alcohol by volume, as this is usually considered the optimum maturation strength. Most whisky is further reduced to 40 per cent before bottling, and this is the legal minimum strength at which Scotch whisky can be sold. There is also a minimum maturation period of three years, although most whisky marketed as single malt will have been matured for at least eight years, in oak casks that have often previously contained sherry or bourbon.

Grain whisky is made predominantly from a variety of cereals, including maize and wheat, all of which are cheaper to buy than the malted barley used to make malt whisky. The stills producing grain spirit can work continuously, whereas malt whisky distilling in pot stills is a 'batch' process, requiring time-consuming cleaning between each period of production. A much greater quantity of grain whisky can therefore be produced in any given period.

Because of the nature of the ingredients and the process of distilling used, the resultant spirit is lacking in strong flavour when compared to the product of a pot still, and it may be the basis for vodka or gin, as well as for producing blended whisky. Although all grain whiskies vary slightly in flavour due to differing cereal recipes, there is not the same range of variables as in malt whisky distillation, and in theory identical grain whisky could be produced on the Hebridean 'whisky island' of Islay and in the heart of Edinburgh.

The processes of mashing and fermenting for grain whisky production are comparable to those for making malt whisky, but grain whisky is distilled in Coffey or 'patent' stills, which consist of two large, connected and parallel columns, called the analyser and rectifier. In essence, what happens in the patent still is that the wash enters at the top and runs over a series of copper plates. As it moves through the still it is met by hot vapour which separates the alcohol from the wash as it travels upwards and enters the condenser at the top of the second or rectifying column. The process is extremely efficient compared to pot still distillation. As with malt spirit, the product of the patent still must, by law, be matured for a minimum of three years before it can be used for blending, or, in rare instances, issued as a 'single grain whisky'.

Some 95 per cent of whisky consumed is in blended form, and the average blended whisky is made up of between a dozen and forty different malts, along with two or three grain whiskies. Once selected, casks of the component malts and grains are poured into a vast blending vat, where compressed air mixes the contents. The newly created blend is then casked for several months to allow all the components to 'marry', though some blenders prefer to keep the marriage of malts and the marriage of grains separate until bottling. Prior to bottling, the blend is reduced with water to market strength, caramel may be added to enhance the colour and ensure its consistency, and filtration usually takes place so that the whisky will not become cloudy when water is added by the consumer.

An ear of barley. Barley is the most vital ingredient in the production of malt Scotch whisky, and while traditionally Scottish barley was used for distilling purposes, now around half of all barley used to make Scotch whisky is imported, mainly from other countries in the EU. The best malting barley has a low nitrogen content, since nitrogen inhibits fermentation, and over the years certain varieties have been developed to provide the optimum distillery yield to whisky-makers.

Pure, whisky-making water. It is often said that distillers favour soft water, rising through peat and flowing over granite, although some excellent whiskies are made using hard water that never encounters either peat or granite. What is essential in 'whisky water' is purity and consistency of supply. The peatiness of the process water will be one factor determining peaty characteristics in the final whisky.

Cutting peat for the maltings of Bowmore distillery, Islay, 1990s. A number of the whiskies produced on the island of Islay are made using malt that is quite heavily peated in the kiln, compared to most mainland malt whiskies. Degrees of peating are measured by ppm (parts per million of phenols), with the highest in Scotland including Ardbeg at up to 50 ppm, while a delicate Speyside may only be peated to one or two ppm.

Taking delivery of a consignment of malting barley at Glenfiddich distillery, Dufftown, Speyside, *c.* 1937. The barley was delivered by the London North-Eastern Railway, either to Dufftown station or to William Grant's own siding nearby. Today, the labour-intensive business of floor-malting has been largely mechanised and centralised, and traditional distillery-based floor-malting is carried on at just a handful of distilleries in Scotland, including Glenfiddich's sister distillery of Balvenie, Highland Park on Orkney, and Bowmore and Laphroaig on the Isle of Islay.

Turning the 'piece', as the bed of barley is known, Benriach distillery, near Elgin, 1982. If the piece is not turned regularly during malting the barley will overheat and germination will cease. Typically, the grain will spend between eight and twelve days on the malting floor until the optimum level of germination is reached.

Firing the kiln, Aberfeldy, 1950s. Burning peat in the kiln gives malted barley influential scents and flavours, though some malt whiskies, such as Glengoyne, are produced using entirely unpeated malt. The most modern maltings do not have a traditional kiln, as a machine was developed during the 1980s that embraces the steeping, germination and kilning processes.

The distinctive 'pagoda' roof of the malt kiln, Balblair distillery, Easter Ross. Today, most distilleries buy in ready-malted barley from specialist companies that prepare it to their individual recipes, so many kilns are now redundant and are retained purely for decorative purposes. The characteristic pagoda roof, as shown, was developed by Charles Doig, the Elgin architect who was responsible for the appearance of so many Speyside distilleries. Doig's design not only looked attractive, but it gave a strong draw to the furnace below, and the first pagoda roof was installed at Dailuaine distillery in 1889.

The tun room, The Glenlivet distillery, 1924. Oregon pine and larch are the traditional materials for washback construction, though stainless steel has replaced wooden vessels in some distilleries, not least because it is so much easier to keep clean. Note the array of overhead pulleys and other apparatus, unacceptable in these days of Health & Safety legislation!

'Switching' a washback at Balvenie, mid-1930s. In the days before the introduction of mechanical 'switchers' into washbacks, the rising wort had to be manually held at bay as the yeast did its work. Modern yeasts tend to make fermentation less volatile than it used to be, and in *Whisky and Scotland*, Highland novelist and former excise officer Neil Gunn wrote, 'I have heard one of those backs rock and roar in a perfect reproduction of a really dirty night at sea.'

The stillhouse, Glenmorangie distillery, Tain, Easter Ross, 1990s. The size, shape and overall design of the stills are some of the most important factors in determining the character of spirit produced. Glenmorangie's stills are very tall, and produce a comparatively light, delicate spirit, as only the lighter alcohols are able to ascend to the top of the still and pass over the lyne arm to be converted from vapour into liquid in condensers.

The stillhouse, Clynelish distillery, Brora, Sutherland, 1980s. Note the contrast in still design with that of Glenmorangie. The malt whisky produced at Clynelish is much more full-bodied. Shorter-necked, more squat stills tend to produce a heavier, more assertive, and even oilier spirit, as heavier alcohols are able to reach the top of the still. Many distillers believe that the best whisky is produced in small stills, and have increased the number of stills rather than made larger ones as demand for their product has grown.

Glenfiddich stillhouse when the stills were heated using coal, 1950s. Today, most stills are heated by oil, gas or steam coils, and only a very few such as Ardmore and Macallan continue to be direct-fired. An average still will last up to fifteen years, but some remain in use much longer, and many are renewed in sections as areas of copper wear thin, rather than being completely replaced.

Spirit safe, Strathisla, 1980s. The brass-bound spirit safe is an eye-catching part of any distillery guided tour, and is a sealed glass tank through which the spirit from the stills passes en route to the spirit receiver. The stillman is able to control the flow of spirit within the safe by separating the early run, or foreshots, and the late run, or feints, from the middle cut, or heart. The heart of the run is the proportion of the distillate that is of the required strength and quality for malt whisky.

Traditional tools of the cooper's trade. Of the many factors that influence the ultimate character of the whisky we drink, few are as important as the cask in which it matures. The cooper is one of the most skilled craftsmen associated with the whisky industry.

The original Speyside Cooperage, Craigellachie, *c.* 1970. The business has been in the hands of the Taylor family since 1947, and in 1992 moved to new, purpose-built premises close to its original site. In a busy year, the cooperage can make some 65,000 casks from new, and repair and reconstruct a further 80,000. The Speyside is one of four cooperages serving the whisky industry in the north-east of Scotland, and boasts an award-winning visitor centre which is very popular with tourists on the Malt Whisky Trail.

Metal cask hoops and wooden staves at the cooperage of the Invergordon grain distillery, Ross-shire. The residual flavours of sherry and bourbon have markedly different effects even on samples of the same malt whisky during maturation, and in recent years there has been a tendency for some distillers to experiment by 'finishing' whiskies matured in American oak for a final year or two in casks that have previously contained port, Madeira or even wine. Thus, the range of variants of even one single malt may have been expanded considerably.

A corner of the Invergordon distillery cooperage. During maturation, the clear, fiery new spirit is tempered by the effects of the sherry or bourbon previously contained in the cask, along with compounds in the wood itself, finally producing a rounded, mellow and complex whisky that has acquired its golden colour in the cask. The most popular sizes of cask used in the Scotch whisky industry are the barrel (40 gallons, 180 litres), the hogshead (55 gallons, 250 litres), and the butt (108 gallons, 490 litres).

Filling casks at The Glenlivet distillery, 1970s. After distillation, the new spirit is piped to the filling store where it is diluted with water before being filled into casks. Today, the 'new make' of many distilleries is taken in bulk by road tankers to centralised filling facilities, and is not matured on site.

Traditional warehousing at The Glenlivet distillery, *c.* 1980. During maturation, spirit matured close to the sea may take on a slightly briny character, and the temperature at which it is stored will affect how much bulk and strength it loses during the process. The excise authorities which police the production and storage of whisky allow for up to 2 per cent of natural evaporation through the porous oak each year. This is known as the 'angels' share'. Today, much modern warehousing lacks the earth flooring featured in this photograph, and casks are stacked high on pallets, accessible only with the use of fork-lift trucks.

The excise office, The Glenlivet distillery, 1924. Since the 1980s, a policy of 'self-policing' by distillers has replaced the former system whereby every distillery in Scotland had at least one resident excise officer whose job it was to ensure the integrity of production at every stage on behalf of the government.

An HM Customs & Excise officer oversees the opening of a bonded warehouse at Glen Grant distillery, Rothes, 1975.

Barley from the steeps being pumped into Saladin boxes for germination, North British grain distillery, Edinburgh, 1998.

Malted barley in a Saladin box, North British distillery, Edinburgh, 1998. The Saladin method is one modern alternative to the hard manual labour of the malting floor. The Saladin box is filled with barley, and a mechanical turner moves backwards and forwards along its length. The North British was one of the first Scottish distilleries to install Saladin boxes during the 1950s, although the process had been developed by a Frenchman during the late nineteenth century.

Mash tun at the North British distillery, 1998. In the mash tun of a grain distillery malted barley and cooked cereal are mixed with water until all the starch has been converted into sugar. The North British is now quite unusual in using maize rather than wheat, along with a high percentage of 'green malt', to create a very distinctive grain spirit.

No. 2 Coffey still, North British distillery, 1998.
The column to the left is the analyser, with the rectifier to the right. A modern Coffey still can distil in the region of 11,000 gallons (50,000 litres) of wash per hour, and remains very similar in design to its earliest predecessors.

Commer lorries from the North British fleet, pictured near Airdrie, late 1950s. When the powerful Distillers Company Ltd (DCL) purchased the Caledonian distillery in Edinburgh in 1884 fears that the firm was developing a stranglehold on grain whisky production led the leading blender Andrew Usher and a number of like-minded merchants and blenders to set up a company to construct their own grain whisky distillery in competition. The result was the North British distillery, located a mile west of the Caledonian in Gorgie. Although some ten distilleries have operated in Edinburgh at various times, only the 'NB' as it is affectionately known, remains in production.

The Caledonian distillery cooperage, 1947. The 'Caly' was founded in 1855, and by the time of its acquisition by DCL was the second largest grain distillery in Britain, situated on a 7.5 acre site in Edinburgh's Haymarket district. The distillery closed in 1988, but its vast chimney still dominates the area, and has been saved from demolition by its 'listed' status. Much of the site has, however, been cleared and redeveloped for residential and commercial use.

Cambus distillery, Tullibody, Clackmannanshire, mid-1930s. Cambus was founded as a malt whisky distillery in 1806, but was converted to distil grain spirit. Cambus was one of the founding distilleries of DCL in 1877, and grew to become one of the largest grain distilleries in Scotland. It was closed by DCL's successor company United Distillers in 1993, and grain whisky production was concentrated on Cameronbridge in Fife and Port Dundas in Glasgow. The warehousing capacity of Cambus is still utilised, and it also functions as a filling store for spirit tankered in from various malt distilleries owned by United Distillers & Vintners, formerly United Distillers.

Cameronbridge distillery, Fife, 1990s. Cameronbridge, at Windygates in Fife, was the first Scottish distillery to produce grain spirit. The distillery was built by members of the Haig family in 1824, and three years later a Stein continuous still was installed. By the 1870s Cameronbridge was producing the astonishing figure of 1.25 million gallons of grain spirit per year. In its modern guise, Cameronbridge is UDVs flagship grain distillery.

Dumbarton distillery, 1980s. The massive, red-brick Dumbarton plant close to the River Clyde was constructed in 1938 by the Canadian distillers Hiram Walker, soon after the company began to expand its activities to Scotland. The distillery stands on the site of a former shipyard, and the grain spirit it produces for its current owners, Allied Distillers, is used in a variety of high-profile blends. Allied also owns the Strathclyde grain distillery in the Gorbals district of Glasgow, while Scotland's newest grain distillery, Loch Lomond, is situated in Alexandria, just a couple of miles north of Dumbarton.

Girvan distillery, Ayrshire, *c.* 1964. William Grant & Sons Ltd built their own grain distillery in 1963 to ensure supplies of grain spirit for their increasingly popular Standfast brand. The distillery is situated on the Ayrshire coast, facing the island of Ailsa Craig and, along with JBB (Greater Europe) plc's Invergordon plant on the Cromarty Firth in the eastern Highlands, it is the only working grain distillery to be located outside the 'Central Belt' of Scotland.

JBB (Greater Europe) plc's Master Blender Richard Paterson at work, 1990s. Paterson is one of the most respected 'noses' in the business, and a third-generation whisky blender. He is responsible for maintaining the standard of blends such as Whyte & Mackay and Claymore, and also creates new blends for JBB clients and for special occasions. According to Paterson, 'What is required is total and utter commitment; one hundred per cent dedication, passion, and pursuit of the highest quality. And time. Whiskies are like people; you get to understand them better as you get older.'

Chivas Master Blender Jimmy Laing (right) prepares to sample spirit, 1969. The average ratio of malt to grain in a blend is between 20 per cent and 60 per cent, though the more deluxe and correspondingly expensive the blended whisky is, the higher the percentage of malt, and the greater the age of the malts included. The character of the casks in which they have been matured will also be a very important consideration for the blender.

The blending room and Dewar's Master Blenders, Perth, 1929. The legendary Canadian distiller Samuel Bronfman, founder of the Seagram empire, declared that 'distilling is a science and blending is an art'. The aim of the blender has been likened to a dinner party host selecting complementary guests for his table. There should be no clashes, all must be harmonious, and the various 'guests' should draw out the best qualities in each other.

Staff at Bell's bottling plant, Perth, *c.* 1904.

Labelling bottles, Glenfiddich bottling hall, 1930s.

Filling cases, Glenfiddich bottling hall, 1930s. Glenfiddich is one of only two Scottish distilleries that continue to bottle on the premises, the other being Springbank in Campbeltown.

Labelling bottles of blended whisky, William Grant's Glasgow warehouse, *c.* 1937. In the background on the left are the vats from which the blended whisky was drawn, and on the right a bottling machine. The company started to blend and bottle in a church basement in the Gorbals district of the city, and this inspired a local rhymester to pen the following doggerel: 'The spirits above were the spirits of love, but the spirits below set the heart aglow.' Later the operation moved to premises beneath the arches of St Enoch's railway station, and in the 1990s a new bottling plant was built on a greenfield site at Bellshill.

'Finishing' a run of 100 Pipers on the production line at Chivas Brothers' newly opened Paisley bottling plant, 1964.

A Drink for the World

White Horse whisky advert from an international promotional campaign, 1992.

In 1908 Sir Robert Usher, son of the blending pioneer Andrew Usher, noted that prior to the effects of the Spirits Act of 1860 only small quantities of Scotch whisky had been sold in England, but that from that date 'the trade in Scotch Whisky increased in leaps and bounds'. Facilitating that increase were representatives of families whose whisky brands are still household names today. They included John and Tommy Dewar, James Buchanan (of Black & White), Alexander Walker (of Johnnie Walker) and Peter Mackie (of White Horse Distillers).

One result of the development of grain whisky had been the growth in influence of the major Lowland distillers who began to specialise in producing grain spirit, and in 1877 Cambus, Cameronbridge, Carsebridge, Glenochil, Kirkliston and Port Dundas amalgamated to form the Distillers Company Ltd. 'DCL', as it was popularly known, was to wield immense power in the Scotch whisky industry for the next 100 years.

The pot still distillers of the Highlands soon began to feel threatened by the dominance of the Lowland operations, and started a campaign to prevent grain and blended whisky from being sold as 'whisky' at all. A considerable amount of spirit retailed as Scotch whisky was unquestionably of poor quality, with malt contributing a modest amount to its contents, while 'ageing' often lasted a matter of months rather than years.

In November 1905 Islington Borough Council prosecuted two wine and spirits merchants for selling goods 'not of the nature, substance and quality demanded' by the provisions of the 1875 Food & Drugs Act. One of the products in question was marketed as 'Fine Old Scotch Whisky', and as its proportions of 90 per cent grain and 10 per cent malt was not an uncommon ratio even with reputable blenders, alarm bells began to ring in the boardroom of DCL and other blending-orientated institutions. Indeed, DCL was so concerned by the possible implications of the prosecution that they funded the merchants' defence.

Islington Borough Council won their case, however, and in 1908 the question of 'What is Whisky?' became the subject of a Royal Commission, which duly reported in July of the following year 'that "whiskey" is a spirit obtained by distillation from a wash saccharified by the diastase of malt, that "Scotch Whiskey" is whiskey as above defined distilled in Scotland'. DCL and their compatriots could breathe a collective sigh of relief. Blended whisky was here to stay.

The thrusting entrepreneurs of the blending trade also received an unexpected boost to their efforts when the louse *phylloxera vastatrix* began to decimate French vineyards during the mid-1860s. Two decades later, Cognac brandy production was almost at a standstill, and Tommy Dewar, Jimmy Buchanan and their ilk were more than happy to step into the breach and offer their wares to accompany the soda in the glasses of English gentlemen, for whom brandy had previously been a staple beverage.

The boom in sales of blended whisky inevitably led to the construction of new distilleries in Scotland and the upgrading and enlargement of many existing plants. Thirty-three new malt whisky distilleries were built during the last decade of the nineteenth century, along with two new grain spirit facilities.

Boom soon to led to bust, however, as the optimism of many eager businessmen who had speculated in whisky proved excessive, and over-production became a feature of the industry. A crisis was precipitated by the collapse in 1899 of the Leith firm of Pattisons

Ltd, headed by the flamboyant Pattison brothers, Robert and Walter. The company failed with liabilities in excess of £500,000 – a very significant sum at the time – and both brothers subsequently served prison sentences for fraud.

The collapse of Pattisons led to a major loss of confidence in the Scotch whisky business, and the 'domino effect' of the firm's demise led to the insolvency of a number of other companies and even the closure of several distilleries.

After work was completed on Glen Elgin distillery in 1900, its designer, Charles Doig, predicted that it would be half a century before a new distillery was constructed in the Scottish Highlands, and two world wars, United States alcohol Prohibition and the interwar depression all conspired to fulfil his prediction.

It was only in the years after the Second World War that the industry began to thrive again, and the first completely new Highland distillery was Tormore, constructed between 1958 and 1960 at Advie, near Grantown-on-Spey. Between 1959 and 1966 malt whisky production rose from 16 million gallons per annum to 51 million gallons, with some distilleries being brought out of mothballs, while many more were significantly expanded and upgraded.

The historical sequence of the 1890s was to be repeated, however, as the end of the 1970s saw a decline in the sales of whisky in Britain and the USA, and the onset of a worldwide recession, which served to blight recently developed export opportunities. The Distillers Company Ltd closed eleven of its forty-five operational malt whisky distilleries in 1983, and a further ten two years later. In all, twenty-nine distilleries fell silent during the first half of the 1980s, as producers sought to lower the levels of the international 'whisky loch'.

Reflecting industry in general, ownership of distilleries has become concentrated into fewer hands during the last half-century, with the Canadian company Seagram being an early foreign investor in Scotch whisky, building a major power-base on Speyside. Fellow Canadian distillers Hiram Walker had started the trend by investing heavily in Scottish distilling during the late 1930s.

More recently, Japanese companies have become important players in the Scotch whisky industry, with Morrison Bowmore Distillers Ltd having been a subsidiary of Suntory, the world's largest distilling company, since 1994. Guinness took over Perth-based Arthur Bell & Sons Ltd in 1986, and the following year acquired DCL amid much controversy, naming the vast new spirits operation United Distillers plc. In 1998 Guinness merged with its largest competitor, Grand Metropolitan, to create Diageo, the largest drinks company in the world. Its spirits division trades as United Distillers & Vintners (UDV). In 2000 a joint venture between UDV and Pernod-Ricard acquired Seagram's wine and spirits operations for £5.5 billion.

Like any business, the Scotch whisky industry does not remain static, and doubtless further amalgamations and programmes of rationalisation will take place, but overall Scotch whisky is performing well in global terms, with export volumes rising by almost 4 per cent during 2000, and the international profile of 'the cratur' has never been higher.

The original premises of John Dewar at 111 High Street, Perth, shortly before their demolition in 1924. John Dewar was born near Aberfeldy in 1805, and joined a relative's wine and spirits business in nearby Perth when he was twenty-three. He went on to open his own premises in Perth High Street in 1846, where ultimately he began to blend and bottle his own whiskies.

Tommy Dewar (1864–1930). Tommy Dewar, youngest son of John, was one of the most flamboyant of the 'whisky barons', and a man who famously set out from his Perth home to spread the gospel of Dewar's blended whisky to London in 1885, aged twenty-one. He went armed with two contacts, one of whom turned out to be bankrupt and the other dead – a setback that in no way dispirited this most tenacious and loquacious of characters – and by the time John Dewar & Sons Ltd merged with the Distillers Company Ltd in 1925 annual profits were running at just under £1.2 million. In 1880 the firm had made a profit of £1,321.

A Dewar's advert dating from 1903. Note the approval of
the medical profession! Other Dewar's adverts stressed the
effectiveness of the brand in protecting the drinker against
flu. After the death of John Dewar senior in 1880, his son
John Alexander took over the running of the company,
with Tommy joining the family firm five years later. John
stayed in Perth, while 'Whisky Tom' travelled the globe,
visiting twenty-six countries and opening thirty-two
agencies during a two-year tour from 1891 to 1893.

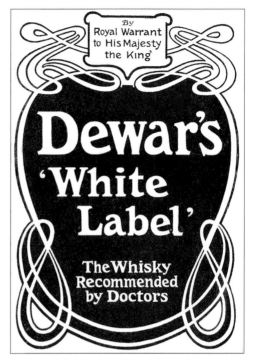

Dewar's East Bond Warehouse, Perth, decorated for the peace celebrations in 1919. The warehouse had been
built seven years previously, when Dewar's transferred their operations from the centre of the city to a large site
adjacent to the main railway line, complete with its own rail sidings. In the early 1960s Dewar's moved again,
this time to a state-of-the-art blending and bottling complex at Inveralmond on the northern outskirts of Perth,
though that facility closed in 1990, and the site was redeveloped, with blending and bottling operations being
centralised to the United Distillers' facility at Leven in Fife.

A Dewar's advert, 1955. Tommy Dewar was knighted in 1901, and in 1919 was elevated to the peerage as Lord Dewar of Homestall in Sussex, three years after his brother John became Lord Forteviot of Duppin, the first of the 'Whisky Barons'. In his role as English country gentleman, Tommy Dewar became an enthusiastic owner and breeder of racehorses, and his Cameronian won the Derby the year after his death, having been left to his nephew, John Arthur, who subsequently became the company chairman.

Arthur Bell, 1880s. Like John Dewar, Arthur Bell joined a Perth wine and spirits company, owned by T.H. Sandeman, in 1840, setting up in his own right eleven years later. He was one of the great pioneers of blending. Bell died in 1900 and was succeeded by his eldest son, Arthur Kinmond, universally known as 'AK'. By this time Bell's was selling well in India, Australia and New Zealand, as well as enjoying strong markets in Europe.

ARTHUR BELL & SONS

ESTAB.ᴰ   1825

OLD SCOTCH WHISKY

PERTH, SCOTLAND.

Bell's label, *c.* 1920 – one of the first to feature the word 'Bell's'. It was not until 1904 that 'AK' commissioned such a label, as his father had forbidden the use of the family name for advertising purposes.

Bell's bottling and packing plant, Perth, 1900. During the 1970s Arthur Bell & Sons followed Dewar's example, and moved its headquarters from the centre of Perth to a new complex at Cherrybank, on the outskirts of the city. The firm remained independent until its takeover by Guinness in 1985, and Cherrybank closed in 1998, when most of the sales, distribution and marketing jobs there were transferred to Harlow in Essex. In 2000, a £2 million Cherrybank Centre was opened to the public, featuring an exhibition charting Bell's long association with Perth.

James Buchanan (1849–1935). Buchanan was another of the blended Scotch pioneers, marketing his 'Buchanan Blend' whisky in an eye-catching black bottle with a white label. He later registered his brand as 'Black & White'. Buchanan was born in Canada, emigrating to Scotland at the age of fourteen. When he was thirty, Buchanan moved to London as agent for the whisky blender Charles Mackinlay, and seeing the potential for sales of a whisky blended specifically to appeal to the English market, he set up his own operation during the mid-1880s.

A Black & White advert, 1938. What was to become the company's trademark logo of a black Scottie and a white West Highland Terrier was James Buchanan's own idea, and it survives on today's bottlings of Black & White whisky. Buchanan was created Lord Woolavington in 1922 and, like Tommy Dewar, he enjoyed the lifestyle of an English country squire. He, too, was a successful breeder of racehorses, twice winning the Derby. When he died in 1935, he left estate valued in excess of £7 million. A decade earlier, James Buchanan & Co. had been absorbed into the DCL empire.

THE WORLD OVER
THEY WILL BE TOASTING CHRISTMAS WITH
"BLACK & WHITE"
BECAUSE *it's the Scotch!*

Peter Mackie (1855–1924). The energetic and frequently irascible Mackie was known as 'Restless Peter', and was memorably described by Sir Robert Bruce Lockhart in his book *Scotch* as 'one-third genius, one-third megalomaniac, one-third eccentric'. Born in Stirling, Mackie learnt the tricks of the whisky trade at his uncle's Lagavulin distillery on Islay before setting up White Horse Distillers in 1880, and beginning to market his famous White Horse brand of blended Scotch.

SCOTCH AND WATER.

A White Horse advert, 1985. Peter Mackie became the third of the so-called 'whisky barons', though in fact he never actually was a baron, being knighted in 1920 by Lloyd George's coalition government. Three years after Mackie's death, White Horse Distillers Ltd joined DCL.

Sir Alexander Walker (1869–1950), grandson of John Walker. The firm of Johnnie Walker & Sons had its origins in John Walker's grocery and wines and spirits business, which had been founded in 1820 in the Ayrshire town of Kilmarnock. Alexander Walker took over the firm on the death of his father (also Alexander) in 1889, and when John Walker & Sons Ltd joined DCL in 1925 Alexander became one of the company's youngest directors. He had been knighted in 1920 for his work during the First World War in the Ministry of Munitions.

Walker's bottling hall, Kilmarnock, 1910. Alexander Walker was probably the most influential figure in the history of the family firm, and was also highly regarded by the entire Scotch whisky industry, controlling as he did the country's largest blending company prior to its loss of independence in 1925. In 1893 Walker's purchased Cardhu (then known as 'Cardow') distillery on Speyside, and three years later added Annandale distillery in south-west Scotland to their portfolio.

A Johnnie Walker advert, 1921. During Sir Alexander Walker's time in charge of the company the now famous slogan 'Johnnie Walker, born 1820 – still going strong' came into use, along with artist Tom Brown's top-hatted 'striding man' figure.

A Johnnie Walker advert, 1957. Recent marketing initiatives have attempted to promote Johnnie Walker as a whisky for the young and image-conscious drinker around the world, and the famous 'striding man' logo has become an altogether 'cooler' character than he used to be.

A Haig whisky advert, 1940s. John Haig & Co. was one of the six founding firms of the Distillers Company Ltd, and the name of Haig goes back a very long way in Lowland Scottish distilling history. In 1655 one Robert Haig of Throst was summoned to appear at the Kirk Session, charged with distilling on the Sabbath. In 1751 Robert's great-great-grandson John married Margaret Stein, a member of another prominent Lowland whisky family, and a name synonymous with the early development of continuous or patent stills half a century later.

A Victorian bottling of 'Haig & Haig Fine Scotch Whisky'. All five of John Haig's sons trained as distillers, and his grandson, also John, built Cameronbridge distillery at Windygates in Fife in 1824. Haig's created a major blending and bottling operation 3 miles from Cameronbridge at Markinch in 1877, though that has now been superseded by a range of modern facilities close by at Leven, designed to embrace most UDV blended brands.

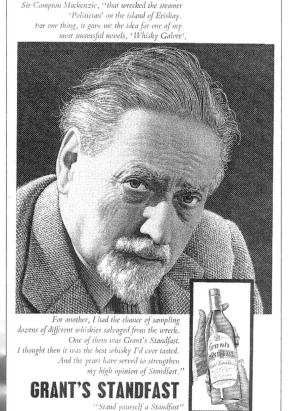

"It was a good wind for me," says Sir Compton Mackenzie, "that wrecked the steamer 'Politician' on the island of Eriskay. For one thing, it gave me the idea for one of my most successful novels, 'Whisky Galore'.

For another, I had the chance of sampling dozens of different whiskies salvaged from the wreck. One of them was Grant's Standfast. I thought then it was the best whisky I'd ever tasted. And the years have served to strengthen my high opinion of Standfast."

GRANT'S STANDFAST

"Stand yourself a Standfast"

Whisky Galore author Compton Mackenzie advertises Grant's Standfast blend, 1958. Mackenzie's comic masterpiece based on the true story of the wrecking of the SS *Politician* off the Hebridean island of Eriskay was published in 1947, and subsequently made into a successful film starring James Robertson Justice, Joan Greenwood and Gordon Jackson.

William Grant & Sons Ltd director John Grant (a grandson of the founder) nosing new make at Balvenie distillery, 1930s. Between 1909 and 1910 William Grant's son-in-law Charles Gordon undertook a marathon overseas promotional tour to market Grant's Standfast blend. He visited India, Malaya, Australia and New Zealand, and by 1914 Grant's had established sixty agencies in thirty different countries.

John Grant examines a ledger, 1930s. Note the advert for Speical Glenfiddich 'pure malt' whisky at a time when most distilleries in Scotland were content just to serve the needs of the blenders.

Loading casks on Lodge Walk, behind Chivas Brothers' King Street shop, Aberdeen, *c.* 1900. Chivas Brothers was yet another company that had its origins in a grocery and wine merchant business. In 1837 James Chivas joined William Edward's Aberdeen firm, and twenty-one years later his brother John became a partner. The company of Chivas Brothers was duly formed.

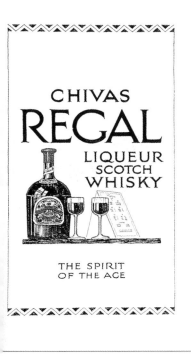

CHIVAS
REGAL
LIQUEUR
SCOTCH
WHISKY

THE SPIRIT
OF THE AGE

By Appointment

CHIVAS
BROTHERS

ABERDEEN

Founded
1801

LIST OF
SCOTCH
WHISKIES
WINES &
CIGARS

TELEGRAMS: "CHIVAS, ABERDEEN"

Chivas Brothers' price list and Chivas Regal advert, 1920s. Chivas Regal was not developed until 1909, after the deaths of both James and John Chivas. From the outset, the deluxe blend was aimed principally at the North American market.

Chivas Brothers advert, 1970s. Note that 1970s icon of Scottish identity, the oil-rig. In 1949 the Canadian firm of Seagram acquired the Chivas company, keen to have the prestigious Chivas Regal brand in their portfolio.

Seagram founder and president Samuel Bronfman at the official opening of Chivas Brothers' new Paisley headquarters and bottling plant, June 1964. The statue of Robert the Bruce is a replica of the one on the battlefield of Bannockburn. Bronfman was keen to have his Scottish headquarters in a castle, and the Seagram HQ in Montreal was a mock Tudor/Gothic construction, complete with portcullis! Bronfman's Scottish architects persuaded him, however, that castles traditionally did not have many windows, and that it would be impossible to produce a realistic working environment in such a structure. Bronfman reluctantly settled for the compromise of an Adam-style country house.

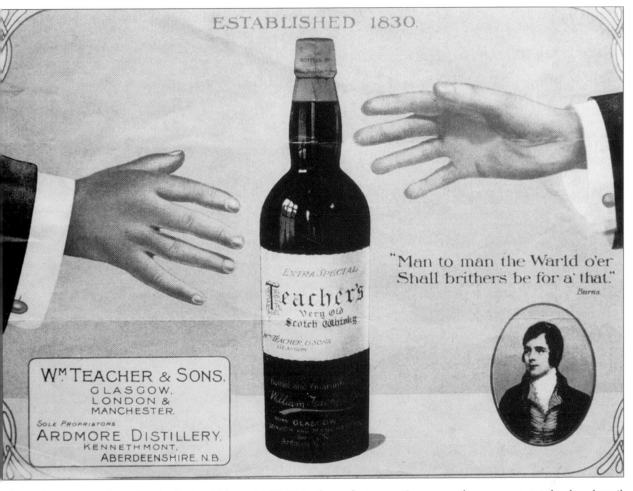

ESTABLISHED 1830.

"Man to man the Warld o'er
Shall brithers be for a' that."

Burns.

EXTRA SPECIAL

Teacher's
Very Old
Scotch Whisky

Wᵐ TEACHER & SONS.
GLASGOW,
LONDON &
MANCHESTER.

SOLE PROPRIETORS
ARDMORE DISTILLERY.
KENNETHMONT,
ABERDEENSHIRE, N.B.

The earliest extant advert for Teacher's whisky, *c.* 1900. Note the cork stopper. Screw-cap closures were not developed until the mid-1920s. In 1884 Teacher's began to market their blended whisky as Highland Cream, and the presentation of the product has changed very little since.

One of the last surviving Teacher's 'dram shops', Cumberland Street, Glasgow, 1950s. William Teacher (1811–76) married a grocer's daughter in the Glasgow district of Anderston, and was instrumental in the grocery shop gaining a licence. By the 1850s the business was thriving, and Teacher introduced the concept of 'dram shops' throughout the city. These were basic but well-run bars, where buying rounds was not allowed in order to cut down on drunkenness, and the only alcohol on sale was Teacher's whisky! The Teacher family built up a chain of eighteen dram shops, making them the largest single licence-holders in the city. The last of the dram shops operated until 1960.

The first official post-Prohibition shipment of Highland Cream leaves Teacher's King Street bottling hall, Glasgow, for the USA, 1934. Although in theory it closed an important market for Scotch whisky, the period of US Prohibition from 1919 to 1933 did not see a complete lack of the spirit in the country. Ingenuity became the watchword, and supplies of Scotch were even fired by torpedoes on to east coast beaches from motor-boats anchored offshore. The 'breaking' of Prohibition had the tacit support of a number of prominent Scotch whisky companies, which did not want the American public to forget the taste of their product.

Delivering Teacher's Highland Cream to licensed premises in London, mid-1970s. As Highland Cream gained in popularity, Teacher's constructed their own Ardmore distillery at Kennethmont in Aberdeenshire to supply malt whisky, and the new plant began to distil in 1899. William Teacher & Sons Ltd refused to succumb to the frequent blandishments of DCL, and remained independent until 1976, when the company was acquired by Allied Breweries, now Allied Distillers.

"Not all Scotch tastes the same!"

Major Hartley W. Whyte, M.B.E., M.C., T.D.
Chairman, Whyte & Mackay Ltd.
Master blender of Scotland's most drinkable Scotch

"Whyte & Mackay tastes better!"

Last year over 1,500,000 bottles of this smooth, subtle Scotch were sold in Scotland alone.
Discover why many Scots prefer Whyte & Mackay. Order Scotland's most drinkable Scotch now!

"Special" The most subtly blended Scotch you can buy—in the bottle with the famous golden measure cap.

"21 Years Old" Every costly drop matured in oak casks for at least 21 years. One of the few really old Scotch whiskies available to the connoisseur.

"Supreme" A superb de luxe Scotch with great strength of character, regal in its elegant decanter.

Whyte & Mackay Limited, Glasgow and London.
An Independent Company Established 1844.

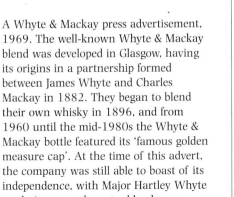

A Whyte & Mackay press advertisement, 1969. The well-known Whyte & Mackay blend was developed in Glasgow, having its origins in a partnership formed between James Whyte and Charles Mackay in 1882. They began to blend their own whisky in 1896, and from 1960 until the mid-1980s the Whyte & Mackay bottle featured its 'famous golden measure cap'. At the time of this advert, the company was still able to boast of its independence, with Major Hartley Whyte as chairman and master blender.

Whyte & Mackay's bottling hall, Glasgow, late 1890s. The company remained independent until 1972, when it was taken over by Sir Hugh Fraser's Scottish & Universal Investments. In 1990 Whyte & Mackay passed to American Brands, makers of Jim Beam bourbon, which in 1993 also took over Invergordon distillers. Five years later they changed the company name to JBB to reflect ownership of their flagship US product. The organisation's Scottish headquarters remains, however, in Glasgow.

During the 'What is Whisky?' case, the Distillers Company Ltd went so far as to market 'light, delicate, exquisite' Cambus grain whisky in bottled format, with a high-profile newspaper advert which mischievously stated that 'Cambus is not a pot still whisky'. They also claimed that it contained 'not a headache in a gallon', a slogan unsustainable in these days of an Advertising Standards Authority!

Opening of the visitor centre, Glenfiddich distillery, 1969. William Grant & Sons were the first distillers actively to encourage visitors to their operation. In 1969 Mrs E.L. Roberts, a granddaughter of William Grant, opened the new reception centre, watched by (from left to right) Sandy Grant Gordon, Managing Director, Eric Roberts, Chairman, and David Grant, Glenfiddich Brand Manager. More than one million people each year now visit the thirty-nine distilleries in Scotland that offer access to the public.

The 'dramming area', Dewar's 'World of Whisky' centre, Aberfeldy distillery, Perthshire, 2000. Dewar's World of Whisky is the ultimate in high-tech, interactive whisky visitor centres, and cost the company some £2 million to develop. It incorporates re-creations of Dewar's old blending room in Perth, where visitors can try their hand at making their own 'virtual' blend, a mock-up of Tommy Dewar's London office, and many examples of Dewar's use of the medium of advertising through the years.

'Donald the Greeter' welcomes customers to Loch Fyne Whiskies' shop, Inveraray, Argyll, 1998. With the recent growth of interest in all aspects of whisky, many specialist outlets such as Richard and Lyndsay Joynson's Loch Fyne Whiskies have sprung up around Scotland, offering an international on-line and mail-order service.

Part of the 'Speyside Malts' display in Fiona Murdoch's Whisky Shop, Dufftown, Speyside, 1990s. Such is the global passion for all things 'whisky' that rare and old bottlings may change hands at auction for sums in excess of £5,000. The shelves of Scottish bookshops contain a growing number of whisky-related volumes, while there are also many websites devoted to the subject. Whisky lovers even have their own dedicated bi-monthly *Whisky Magazine*.

The barrel ride, Scotch Whisky Heritage Centre, Castlehill, Edinburgh. The Scotch Whisky Heritage Centre makes an ideal starting point for anyone wishing to discover more about Scotland's national drink before setting off to see distilleries for themselves. One attraction is a tour through the centuries of Scotch whisky history in electronically driven 'barrel-cars', featuring life-like figures, sounds, and even aromas. Such is the overseas interest in Scotch whisky that tours are available in eight languages.

The Whisky Museum, Dufftown. At the opposite end of the 'high-tech' spectrum to the Scotch Whisky Heritage Centre and Dewar's 'World of Whisky', Dufftown's Whisky Museum is based in a former undertaker's shop, and operates with voluntary staff. It features fascinating artefacts and documents from the 'Whisky Capital's past, and provides a focal point for whisky-related activities in the Speyside town. The illicit still in the left-hand window display was discovered (not working) in Mortlach distillery, while the spirit safe on the right was removed from Banff distillery when it closed in 1983.

The heart of a modern distillery, Braes of Glenlivet, 1970s. Along with its sister distillery of Allt a Bhainne, Braes of Glenlivet (now re-christened Braeval) is highly automated, and designed to be operated by just one man per shift. During recent years, many older distilleries have also been adapted to operate on a much less labour-intensive basis and thereby cut staff costs, though sadly the effect of job losses on small rural distilling communities can be severe.

The evolution of the whisky bottle, 1844–1998, courtesy of Whyte & Mackay. The Whyte & Mackay bottle remained remarkably unchanged for many years, until the company took the radical step of making the principal label colour blue in 1998, reflecting the growing importance of branding and marketing in the whisky industry. Many distillers who had long used brown or green bottles switched to clear glass in order to emphasise the attractive colour of their product.

Four examples of whisky-related Scottish postcard humour, early twentieth century. 'Saxpence winna bang noo' means 'sixpence won't buy anything now'. Along with tartan, alleged parsimony, and the Loch Ness Monster, whisky has provided a cliché of Scottish life that has been both a blessing to the Scotch whisky industry and also a curse, when it comes to attracting new and younger drinkers.

In their perpetual attempt to capture the youth market and distance themselves somewhat from the traditional images associated with the spirit, Scotch whisky companies have become involved in some unlikely sponsorship projects. Here, Queen Anne whisky does its bit for 1970s motorbike combination racing.

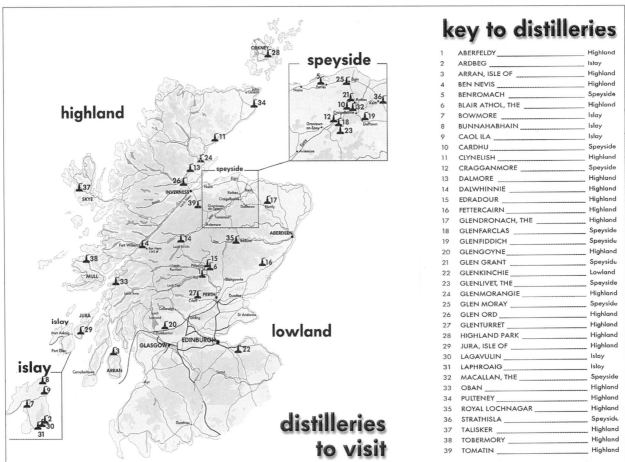

key to distilleries

1	ABERFELDY	Highland
2	ARDBEG	Islay
3	ARRAN, ISLE OF	Highland
4	BEN NEVIS	Highland
5	BENROMACH	Speyside
6	BLAIR ATHOL, THE	Highland
7	BOWMORE	Islay
8	BUNNAHABHAIN	Islay
9	CAOL ILA	Islay
10	CARDHU	Speyside
11	CLYNELISH	Highland
12	CRAGGANMORE	Speyside
13	DALMORE	Highland
14	DALWHINNIE	Highland
15	EDRADOUR	Highland
16	FETTERCAIRN	Highland
17	GLENDRONACH, THE	Highland
18	GLENFARCLAS	Speyside
19	GLENFIDDICH	Speyside
20	GLENGOYNE	Highland
21	GLEN GRANT	Speyside
22	GLENKINCHIE	Lowland
23	GLENLIVET, THE	Speyside
24	GLENMORANGIE	Highland
25	GLEN MORAY	Speyside
26	GLEN ORD	Highland
27	GLENTURRET	Highland
28	HIGHLAND PARK	Highland
29	JURA, ISLE OF	Highland
30	LAGAVULIN	Islay
31	LAPHROAIG	Islay
32	MACALLAN, THE	Speyside
33	OBAN	Highland
34	PULTENEY	Highland
35	ROYAL LOCHNAGAR	Highland
36	STRATHISLA	Speyside
37	TALISKER	Highland
38	TOBERMORY	Highland
39	TOMATIN	Highland

distilleries to visit

A Scotch Whisky Association map showing the distribution of distilleries with visitor facilities, 2001.

The Malt Whisky
Distilleries of Scotland

Workers on the pier at Lagavulin distillery, Islay, 1912.

At the time of writing, there are in excess of eighty operational distilleries in Scotland making malt whisky and a further eight producing grain spirit. The malt whisky distilleries are to be found from the Orkney islands in the north to Galloway in the deep south-west, and their locations have principally been dictated by the local availability of the 'raw materials' essential for malt whisky distilling. These include barley, a guaranteed supply of pure water, and peat or coal to produce heat and power.

With the development of the railway network during the second half of the nineteenth century, proximity to a railway line became another factor borne in mind by distillery developers, for whom the potential to import barley and coal and export casks of spirit by train was highly attractive. Accessibility may have had great advantages, but many of today's distilleries are found in comparatively remote and inaccessible areas. In days gone by, remoteness could be just as priceless an asset as a favourable water supply if the distiller happened, as was often the case, to be operating without the benefit of a licence. A considerable number of modern distilleries have their origins in illicit operations that were active two centuries and more ago.

Scotch malt whisky distilleries are customarily divided into a number of geographical 'regions' and even 'sub-regions' for purposes of discussion and analysis, with the principal classifications usually being 'Highland', 'Speyside', 'Island', 'Islay', 'Campbeltown' and 'Lowland'.

The first division between distilleries was for fiscal reasons, with a theoretical 'Highland Line' being introduced in 1784 (see Introduction) when differing rates of excise duty began to be levied in the Highlands and the Lowlands.

Today, the various whisky regions serve to identify distilleries geographically, and also to suggest vague stylistic similarities, though this can be a dangerous line to pursue too dogmatically, since it is not impossible to find a Speyside whisky that could easily be from the Lowlands, and an Islay that could be a Highlander!

The Highland classification of distilleries is the largest in physical area, and also the most difficult to generalise about in terms of style, as it encompasses malts produced on both the east and west coasts, as well as in the northern, central and southern Highlands.

'Speyside' came to merit a category of its own during the latter part of the nineteenth century, when the blending revolution brought its style of complex, elegant, mellow malt whiskies into particular favour, and the whisky-making capacity of the region expanded dramatically. No fewer than twenty-one of the thirty-three new distilleries that opened during the last decade of the century were located on Speyside. Today, more than half of the country's working distilleries are in the region, and the dozen malts categorised by blenders as 'top class' are all Speysides. The offical 'Malt Whisky Trail' on Speyside encourages visitors to experience tours of a variety of distilleries, along with the Speyside Cooperage at Craigellachie and the whisky heritage centre in the now silent Dallas Dhu distillery near Forres, operated under the auspices of Historic Scotland.

Single malts from Islay are unquestionably the most assertive and distinctive of all Scotch whiskies, and from at least the late eighteenth century whiskies produced on Islay have been noted for their individuality of flavour. Their style owes much to the vast areas of peat that are such a feature of the Hebridean island, and which influence the whisky process water that flows through them, giving 'briny' as well as 'smoky' characteristics to the finished whisky. In addition to being highly prized as single malts, the whiskies of Islay play a modest but vital role in many blends, which may well explain the island's enduring success as a whisky-making region.

The long, mainland peninsula of Kintyre lies just a few miles east of Islay, and it, too, was an ideal place for whisky-making, owing to ready access to peat and water, an excellent harbour at Campbeltown, and remoteness when distilling outwith the law required it.

When Alfred Barnard visited the fishing port of Campbeltown at the southern end of the Argyllshire peninsula during the 1880s, he proclaimed it 'whisky city', touring twenty-one distilleries in the borough. By 1925, however, just a dozen Campbeltown distilleries were working, and by the end of 1934 only Glen Scotia and Springbank remained. Both keep the Campbeltown distilling tradition alive today.

A number of factors led from boom to bust for the 'whisky city', not least the increasing popularity during the late nineteenth century of Speyside malts with blenders. Some Campbeltown distillers had also been less than scrupulous regarding the quality of their whisky as they attempted to undercut the competition around the turn of the century, which irreparably damaged the reputation of Campbeltown's make. The period of US Prohibition from 1919 to 1933 had a serious effect on one of Campbeltown's principal markets, and by that time poor road links with Glasgow were also beginning to take their toll.

Lowland whiskies have long been regarded as the poor relations of the single malt world, although many of the characteristically light-bodied, aperitif whiskies that have been produced in the region are actually excellent drams.

Legal distilling is recorded as having taken place at more than 300 sites in what we would term the 'Lowland' region, which includes the cities of Edinburgh and Glasgow. It was reported in 1777 that some 400 stills were operating in the Scottish capital, though sadly for the collectors of excise, only eight of them held licences!

When the blending revolution came along, virtually all the output from Lowland stills was absorbed into the blending vats, and even the growth of interest in single malts during the past two decades tends to have passed the Lowlanders by. Today, only three productive Lowland distilleries survive, though the area is still the principal source of Scottish grain whisky.

It is important to bear in mind that several hundred legal distilleries have operated in Scotland and are now no more. Many have disappeared without trace beneath housing or industrial developments, and others lie in ruins, while some have been re-developed and found new leases of life. The pages that follow feature images of distilleries captured at various times during the past century: they portray a mixture of those that are still working today, some that are now long silent, and others that are no more than distant memories.

i
HIGHLAND

Ben Morven Distillery, Halkirk, Caithness, *c.* 1900. Ben Morven had its origins in an earlier plant that operated under the name of Gerston from 1796 until 1875. The distillery pictured was constructed a decade later, and it too initially traded as Gerston. By the turn of the century, however, it had been rechristened Ben Morven, though nobody had got around to repainting the roof! Ben Morven ceased production before the First World War, and today there is little evidence of its existence.

Filling casks, Pulteney distillery, 2000. Pulteney is situated in the Caithness fishing port of Wick, and is the northernmost mainland distillery in Scotland. It was founded in 1826, when Wick was at the centre of the thriving herring fishing industry. The distillery was silent from 1930 to 1951, and in 1959 underwent an unflattering programme of reconstruction while in the ownership of Canadian distilling company Hiram Walker, which meted out a similarly brutal treatment to Scapa on Orkney.

The visitor centre, Pulteney distillery, 2000. In 1995, Pulteney was acquired by Inver House Distillers Ltd, who proceeded to invest in the fabric of the distillery, creating an attractive visitor centre that emphasises the maritime heritage of the town of Wick. An energetic promotional campaign has ensured that the slightly salty, elegant and previously underrated Old Pulteney single malt is now much easier to find in off-licences and supermarkets than used to be the case.

The original Clynelish distillery, Brora, east Sutherland, 1990s. Clynelish was founded in 1819 by the Marquis of Stafford to provide employment and a use for barley grown by crofters on his estate. During the 1960s, DCL constructed a new distillery next to Clynelish in order to increase capacity, and the old plant subsequently fell victim to the company's 1983 round of distillery closures. It remains, externally at least, intact. Stylistically, Clynelish single malt is surprising, being sufficiently powerful, peaty and iodine-flavoured that it could almost be an Islay, though recent bottlings are more subdued than those of a few years ago.

Balblair distillery, Edderton, Ross-shire, 1980s. One of five operational distilleries that line the shores of the neighbouring Cromarty and Dornoch Firths, Balblair was built alongside the main Highland Railway line in 1895. This traditional plant is currently operated by Inver House Distillers Ltd, a firm that has made something of a habit of buying up distilleries considered to be surplus to larger companies' requirements and marketing the single malts with notable success, as in the case of Pulteney. Thanks to Inver House, the once almost unobtainable Balblair single malt is now considerably easier to find.

The stillhouse, Glenmorangie, Tain, 1990s. Glenmorangie distillery stands beside the Dornoch Firth and was founded in 1843 on the site of an ancient brewery. In 1887, a programme of renovation and expansion was undertaken, and the plant's capacity has subsequently been increased on several occasions. The latest stillhouse is home to eight stills, which, at almost 17ft, are the tallest pot stills in Scotland, and their shape and size is based on the original stills installed during the 1840s, which were purchased second-hand from a London gin distillery. Glenmorangie is delicate and medium-bodied, with a fine, flowery aroma, and is Scotland's best-selling single malt.

Dalmore distillery, Alness, 1993. Dalmore is situated on the shores of the Cromarty Firth, and traces its history back to 1839 when it was founded by the tea and opium trader Alexander Matheson. The Mackenzie Brothers owned Dalmore from 1878 until 1960, when they amalgamated with Whyte & Mackay Ltd, now part of JBB (Greater Europe) plc. The company's Invergordon grain distillery is located just a couple of miles further along the Firth from Dalmore. During the First World War Dalmore distillery was used as a factory for the manufacture of deep-sea mines, with the result that an explosion necessitated substantial postwar rebuilding.

Glen Albyn and the Caledonian Canal, Inverness, 1957. Distilling is recorded as having taken place on at least a dozen sites in the Highland capital of Inverness, where three working distilleries survived until the 1980s. Glen Albyn dated from 1844, and in 1892, during the 'whisky boom', a new 'sister' distillery called Glen Mhor was built on a neighbouring site. While the make of both distilleries was principally used for blending, Glen Mhor was also respected as a single malt. Both distilleries fell victim to DCL cuts during the 1980s, and have disappeared entirely beneath modern retail developments.

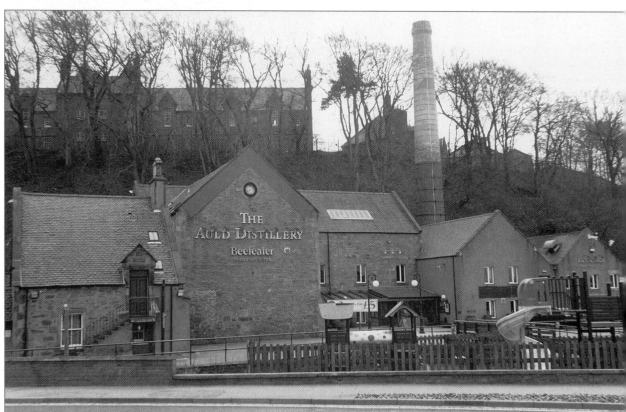

The former Millburn distillery, Inverness, 2001. Millburn was founded around 1807, and was substantially rebuilt in 1876. The distillery buildings that remain at the core of the 'Auld Distillery' restaurant and pub development date from that time. Millburn fell silent in 1985, when in the ownership of DCL, and its single malt is now very elusive, though in its day it was as well regarded as Glen Mhor, with a slightly peaty and quite smoky house style.

Ben Nevis distillery, Lochy Bridge, Fort William, late nineteenth century, with Scotland's highest mountain in the background. Along with UDV's Oban plant, Ben Nevis is the only distillery operating in the western Highlands today, and historically there have been surprisingly few legal whisky-making operations in the area. Their scarcity is probably due to the fact that the terrain of the west is less conducive to the cultivation of malting barley than that of the eastern and north-eastern Highlands. Ben Nevis was founded by 'Long John' Macdonald in 1825, but has been in the ownership of the Japanese whisky firm Nikka since 1989.

Glenlochy distillery, Fort William, with Loch Linnhe in the background, 1930s. Glenlochy was founded in 1898 and, like Ben Nevis, was once owned by the colourful Canadian-born millionaire Joseph Hobbs, who had made his money in property and shipbuilding, and became a distiller and cattle rancher in the Great Glen, which runs north-east between Fort William and Inverness. Glenlochy was acquired by DCL in 1953, but its make was always best used for blending, and it closed thirty years later. The maltings and kilns are listed and have survived, while much of the rest of the distillery has been demolished.

Dalwhinnie distillery, 1990s. Dalwhinnie distillery is the highest in Scotland, standing 1,164 feet above sea level in Inverness-shire. Dalwhinnie is located almost due east of Fort William, and is situated in spectacularly bleak country just off the A9 Perth–Inverness road. The distillery opened in 1898 under the name of Strathspey, and its make is now one of UDV's six 'Classic Malts'. From 1895 to 1911 a distillery operated in the nearby village of Kingussie under the name of Speyside, and when that plant ceased trading, its condensing 'worm tub' was purchased by Dalwhinnie, where it remained in use until the mid-1980s.

Detail from the entrance gate at Blair Athol distillery, Pitlochry, Perthshire, 1990s. Although founded in 1798, the present distillery actually dates from 1826, and following its acquisition by Arthur Bell & Sons in 1933 it was substantially rebuilt. Production did not recommence, however, until healthier economic conditions prevailed in the years following the Second World War. The distillery's capacity was doubled from two to four stills in 1973, and today, under UDV ownership, the site incorporates an impressive visitor centre, which traces the history of the distillery and the Bell's dynasty of blenders.

Edradour distillery, near Pitlochry, 1990s. Edradour was founded in 1825, and has changed remarkably little since that time. As Scotland's smallest working distillery, Edradour's output of spirit fills around a dozen casks, or 3,500 bottles, per week, which means that its annual production is equal to one week's make at an average Speyside distillery. As no more than 2,000 cases of Edradour single malt are released each year, this fine creamy, honeyed whisky can be quite elusive.

Aberfeldy distillery, Perthshire, soon after its opening in 1898. Aberfeldy was built by the Dewar family to guarantee supplies of malt for their increasingly popular blended whiskies. Today, it is owned by Bacardi-Martini. One important factor in the siting of Aberfeldy distillery was its proximity to the railway line linking Aberfeldy to Perth, where the company's blending and bottling operations were based. Note the distillery workers rolling casks filled with Aberfeldy single malt down to the railway line, seen in the bottom right corner of the picture.

Glenturret distillery, Crieff, Perthshire, 1990s. Glenturret claims to be Scotland's oldest distillery, tracing its origins to 1775, and it now receives more visitors than any other in the country. Like so many distilleries, Glenturret closed during the recession of the 1920s, but unlike most, it reopened after being acquired and re-equipped by businessman and whisky enthusiast James Fairlie during the late 1950s. It is now owned by Highland Distillers plc.

Glenturret's former distillery cat, Towser. Towser lived in the stillhouse from 1963 until 1987, during which time she despatched 28,899 mice, earning her an entry in the *Guinness Book of Records* as World Mousing Champion. Towser is commemorated with her very own statue next to the distillery visitor centre.

Glengoyne distillery, 1990s. Glengoyne is situated a dozen miles north of Glasgow at Killearn, and stands in the shadow of Dumgoyne Hill (right). According to legend, the Highland Line separating Highland from Lowland distilleries actually passes through the Glengoyne site, so that although the whisky is distilled in the Highlands, it matures in the Lowlands on the other side of the A81 road! Until the 1970s, Glengoyne was often classified as a Lowland malt. The distillery was first licensed in 1833, and many of the current buildings date from a 1966/67 rebuild. Its single malt whisky is made using entirely unpeated malt.

The staff, Fettercairn distillery, Angus, 2001. Fettercairn distillery is situated at the foot of the Cairngorms, near Laurencekirk, in an area that was once a hotbed of illicit distilling. It dates from 1824, but was rebuilt in the late 1880s after a fire, undergoing a further programme of extension and reconstruction in 1966, when its capacity was doubled by the introduction of a new pair of stills. Fettercairn belongs to JBB (Greater Europe) plc, and is a component of Whyte & Mackay blends.

Glenury Royal distillery, Stonehaven, 1960s. Along with Brackla at Nairn and Lochnagar, Glenury was one of only three Scottish distilleries to be granted use of the word 'royal', and this historic distillery was established in 1825 by local Member of Parliament Captain Robert Barclay. While Brackla and Lochnagar remain productive, Glenury – in the ownership of DCL – fell silent in 1985 and, in 2000, demolition began to make way for a housing development.

Lochside distillery, Montrose, 1990s. One of the most architecturally distinctive distilleries in Scotland, Lochside began life as a brewery, constructed in Bavarian 'brauhaus' style during the 1890s. It was converted to a distillery in 1957, and last made whisky in 1992, when it was closed by Allied Distillers, who found it surplus to their requirements. Although Lochside's warehousing has been demolished, the principal distillery buildings remain intact, with distilling plant *in situ*, though development plans for the site mean that Lochside is unlikely to survive much longer. The dry, fruity single malt is elusive, but highly regarded.

ii

SPEYSIDE

A detail of Glen Moray distillery, Elgin, 1990s. Glen Moray was originally built as Henry Arnot's brewery, becoming a distillery in 1897, when the 'whisky boom' was at its height.

The Clocktower, Dufftown, 1990s. If Speyside is the whisky heartland of Scotland, then Dufftown is its capital. The town in its present form dates from 1817, when it was laid out by James Duff, the 4th Earl of Fife. For centuries, the area around Dufftown was a hotbed of illicit distilling, and legend has it that at one time an illicit still operated in the clocktower, under the noses of the town's excise officers!

Dufftown is famous far and near,
    And many days are 'letter'd red',
The very spot for Holidays,
    And who comes now but good King Ned.
        G.R.

The king visits the Capital of malt whisky. This visit to Dufftown by Edward VII (r. 1901–10), believed to have been in 1907, took place during one of his regular autumn stays with the Sassoon family at Tulchan Lodge, near Grantown-on-Spey. Dufftown's first distillery was Mortlach, which was founded in 1823, but as the town developed rapidly as a whisky-making centre during the 1890s, an anonymous scribbler penned the rhyme 'Rome was built on seven hills, and Dufftown stands on seven stills'.

Staff photograph, Mortlach distillery, Dufftown, 1885. William Grant (1839–1923) was manager at the time, and is seen on the extreme left. Grant started work at Mortlach as a book-keeper at the age of twenty-seven, and by the mid-1880s he had saved enough money to take the plunge and build his own distillery, using equipment purchased second-hand from Cardow (now known as Cardhu). Grant was determined that he would produce spirit at his new plant during the Queen's Golden Jubilee year, and he just managed to do so, with the first spirit flowing from Glenfiddich on Christmas Day 1887.

Glenfiddich distillery, 1930s. Glenfiddich was only the second distillery to be built in Dufftown, and it is now one of the most productive malt whisky distilleries in Scotland. The number of stills may have increased, but each one is still modelled on the originals purchased from Cardow, and William Grant & Sons Ltd remains an independent company with a significant family involvement. Glenfiddich is a comparatively light-bodied Speyside, with a gentle character.

Transferring casks of mature malt whisky from a bonded warehouse to a railway truck, Glenfiddich, 1930s. Glenfiddich distillery was one of many to take advantage of railways for the swift transportation of raw materials and casks of whisky. The Keith to Dufftown railway line, which opened in 1862 and was latterly unused for many years, has recently been restored to its former glory by volunteers from the Keith and Dufftown Railway Association, and trains once again run along its 11 miles of track.

Loading a lorry with cases of Glenfiddich single malt, Glenfiddich distillery, 1950s. William Grant & Sons was one of the first companies to see the potential for sales of single malt whisky in a market dominated by blends, and since the late 1950s they have promoted Glenfiddich with great ability and tenacity. In a now crowded market place, Glenfiddich remains the best-selling single malt both in Britain and abroad.

Balvenie distillery, 1930s. Such was the success of William Grant's Glenfiddich venture that five years after its founding he constructed the Balvenie distillery on a neighbouring site, again showing a shrewd eye for a bargain, by equipping the new distillery with stills purchased from Glen Albyn in Inverness and Lagavulin on Islay. Note the 'worm tubs' on the right, beside the stillhouse. The vapours from the stills entered at the top, condensing as they passed down through the coiled metal 'worm', immersed in cold water. In many distilleries, condensers attached to the still necks have now replaced worm tubs.

Parkmore distillery, Dufftown, 1990s. Parkmore was built during the great distilling boom of the 1890s, but production ceased in 1931, just six years after the distillery had been acquired by DCL. Despite seven decades of silence, Parkmore remains externally one of the finest examples of undeveloped late Victorian distillery architecture in existence, and owes its survival to the fact that its extensive warehousing capacity has long been useful to its owners.

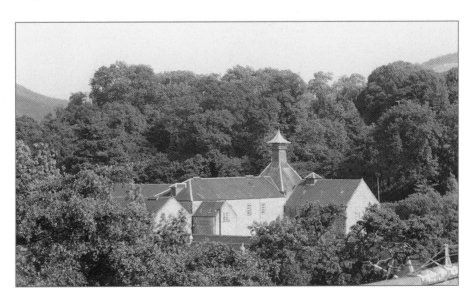

One of the stills, Macallan distillery, Easter Elchies, 1990s.
The Macallan distillery was established in 1824, and produces one o
Scotland's most highly regarded single malts. The whisky is distilled
in the smallest direct-fired stills in Scotland, using Golden Promise
barley, and is matured exclusively in ex-sherry wood. The Macallan
stills are much smaller than one might imagine, considering the
output of the plant, which has the capacity to produce around
2 million proof gallons of spirit per year. Like Glenfiddich, Macallan
has resisted the temptation to increase the capacity of their stills
and has instead increased their number, which now stands at
twenty-one.

Macallan Master Distiller David
Robertson sampling spirit in a
Macallan warehouse. When he
took over the running of The
Macallan in 1994, David was
the youngest distillery manager
in Scotland. He notes,
'Fortunately, whisky-making is
still an art – it has yet to
become a science – and it is this
specific aspect of craft and
tradition that makes the job so
varied and interesting. No one
will ever be able to improve on
the human nose and intellect
for determining how our
maturing spirit, each sherry
cask with different hints of
cloves, raisins, prunes, wood,
toffee, cinnamon, pears, apricot
and ginger should be married
together to make The Macallan.'

James Grant (1847–1931) fly-fishing in the Highlands. Glen Grant distillery is one of five plants in the little town of Rothes, and was founded by brothers John and James Grant in 1840; it was James's son (pictured) who shaped the present-day operation, expanding what was already one of the largest whisky-making plants in Scotland. 'The Major', as James Grant was universally known, lived the life of a Highland laird, fishing and hunting, while he also travelled widely in Africa and India. At the age of seventy-four he caught no fewer than thirty-eight salmon and grilse in a single fishing expedition.

One of a series of 1970s adverts for Glen Grant single malt, for which drawings were commissioned by leading cartoonists of the day, in this case Honeysett. Glen Grant was being bottled and sold as a single malt in the early years of the twentieth century when few other distillers were retailing anything but blends. Younger expressions of the whisky are now extremely popular in European markets, having a notably strong following in Italy. Just what 'The Major' would have made of such irreverent advertising remains a matter of conjecture!

Biawa Makalaga in the uniform of the Northamptonshire Regiment, *c.* 1916. During a visit to Matebeleland in 1898, James Grant's hunting party found two orphaned boys in the care of a poor local cattle-herder. The Major brought one of the children home to Rothes, where he educated him and gave him a job, ultimately as his butler. In 1916 Biawa was called up for military service, and joined the Northamptonshire Regiment, then based at Fort George barracks near Inverness. After war service he returned to Rothes, where he died in his mid-eighties in 1972.

Speyburn distillery, 1990s. Speyburn is beautifully situated on the northern outskirts of Rothes, and is most people's idea of what a Scottish distillery ought to look like. Speyburn was built during 1897, the year of Queen Victoria's Diamond Jubilee and so keen were its owners to have fillings of their new whisky with the jubilee date on it that stillhouse staff were obliged to wear coats while they worked in an unfinished building that lacked doors and windows during the last, freezing days of December! Having become surplus to DCL requirements, Speyburn was purchased by Inver House Distillers Ltd in 1991.

Longmorn distillery staff, 1923. Longmorn was founded in 1894 by the Longmorn Distillery Company, and is situated close to the main Rothes to Elgin A941 road. Three years after its opening, the 'Glenlivet' suffix was added to the distillery name, in common with many other Speyside distilleries not actually in the famous glen, as can be seen on the cask stencilling in this picture. In 1970, Longmorn and its sister distillery of Benriach became part of the Glenlivet Distillers Ltd, and in 1977 passed to Seagram.

Longmorn distillery staff, 1980. This photograph features the Ruston 'puggie' engine used to haul casks round the Longmorn site, and was taken shortly before the engine left the distillery and found a 'retirement' home at the Strathspey Railway at Boat of Garten. Longmorn is regarded by blenders as one of the leading Speyside malts, and is also bottled as a 'single' by its proprietors, now without the Glenlivet suffix. Independent bottlers, however, continue to label it as Longmorn-Glenlivet.

Strathisla distillery, 1930s. Strathisla is one of three distilleries situated in the Banffshire town of Keith, which also boasts several more such as Aultmore and Glentauchers in its environs. Strathisla dates from 1786, and was originally known as Milltown, with the Strathisla name being used during the 1870s and '80s, then again from the 1950s, after the distillery had become one of Seagram's first Scottish acquisitions. Today it is one of the company's showpiece plants with an attractive visitor centre, and the sweet, spicy, full-bodied single malt is a significant component of the Chivas Regal blend.

Redundant spirit still, Glenfarclas distillery, Ballindalloch, 2001. Situated close to the main A95 road, near Aberlour, Glenfarclas boasts the largest pot stills on Speyside, and remains one of the few family-owned distilleries to have survived the pressures of takeovers, amalgamations and consolidations that have been such a feature of the whisky industry during the twentieth century. The managing director John Grant is the great-great-grandson of John Grant, who took on the distillery in 1865, some thirty years after an initial licence was granted.

The Glenlivet distillery, Minmore, 1924. The present Glenlivet distillery dates from the late 1850s, and the spirit it produces is a classic Speyside; quite sweet and lightly sherried, with notes of peat. The operation has its origins in a still run by George Smith at nearby Upper Drumin Farm – the first still to be granted a licence in the wake of the 1823 Excise Act. The remoteness of Glenlivet made it a haven for illicit distilling, and it was, rather improbably, estimated that at the close of the eighteenth century no fewer than 200 illegal stills were operating in the glen.

Redundant stills, The Glenlivet, 1980s. Riveted stills such as these are a great rarity today, with welding having long since superseded the practice of riveting. By the 1880s, so many distilleries were using the 'Glenlivet' name that John Smith instigated legislation in an attempt to protect the integrity of his whisky. The result was an agreement that only G. & J.G. Smith were allowed to use the definite article in front of the Glenlivet name. Other distillers could, however, use 'Glenlivet' as a hyphenated addition to their own distillery titles. At one time, twenty-eight distilleries chose to incorporate the Glenlivet suffix.

George Smith's descendant Bill Smith Grant (1896–1975) presents a bottle of The Glenlivet single malt to Prime Minister Edward Heath, during a visit by the premier to the distillery in September 1972. Bill Smith Grant became proprietor of The Glenlivet distillery in 1921, and during his time at the helm of the company of G&JG Smith the Glenlivet operation grew immensely, amalgamating with J&J Grant, Glen Grant Ltd in 1952, and going on to become The Glenlivet Distillers Ltd in 1970, when Longmorn-Glenlivet Distilleries Ltd and the blenders and bottlers Hill Thomson & Co. Ltd were also incorporated.

Construction in progress on Allt-a-Bhainne distillery, which came on stream in 1975, two years after its sister distillery of Braes of Glenlivet. The two distilleries were designed to be operated by one man per shift, and their spirit was always destined for the blending vats producing Chivas blends such as Chivas Regal, Passport, and 100 Pipers.

Braes of Glenlivet distillery, soon after completion in 1973. Braes of Glenlivet was built by Seagram prior to their acquisition of The Glenlivet distillery in 1977, and its naming was a clear attempt to associate themselves with the prestige of 'Glenlivet'. Once the company took over The Glenlivet, however, Braes of Glenlivet was re-christened Braeval, so as not to diminish the Glenlivet cachet. Braeval stands in a very remote location near the hamlet of Chapeltown, and is one of only four distilleries actually located in the parish of Glenlivet.

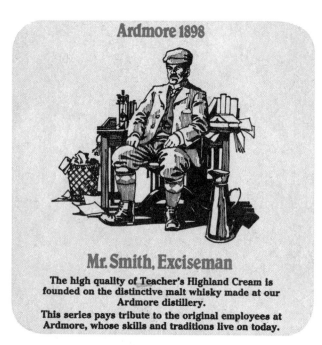

Ardmore 1898

Mr. Smith, Exciseman

The high quality of Teacher's Highland Cream is founded on the distinctive malt whisky made at our Ardmore distillery.

This series pays tribute to the original employees at Ardmore, whose skills and traditions live on today.

A Teacher's drink-mat advert, 1980s. Ardmore distillery opened in 1898 at Kennethmont in Aberdeenshire, on the eastern fringes of Speyside, and was constructed by William Teacher & Sons Ltd to provide malt whisky for the firm's expanding blending business. More than a century after its opening, Ardmore's spirit is still a significant component of Teacher's Highland Cream, and remains elusive as a single malt. A distinctive feature of this large distillery is the fact that the stills remain direct-fired, rather than heated by steam. Ardmore is surprisingly smoky and peaty for a Speysider, and is one of the region's better-kept secrets.

Tormore distillery, Advie, 1980s. Tormore is a bold, confident architectural statement, which sits well among its older and more traditional Speyside neighbours. The distillery is situated at the foot of the Cromdale Hills, beside the main A95 road between Grantown-on-Spey and Bridge of Avon, and dates from 1958/60. Tormore was designed by the eminent architect Sir Albert Richardson, and was the first entirely new distillery to be built in the Highlands during the twentieth century. Since 1990 it has belonged to Allied Distillers.

iii

THE ISLANDS

Highland Park distillery, Kirkwall, Orkney, 1990.

Maltings staff, Highland Park, 1990s. Highland Park, situated on the outskirts of Kirkwall, is the northernmost distillery in Scotland. Now owned by Highland Distillers plc, it was founded in 1798 and remains very traditional in its working practices. Highland Park continues to make some of its own malt using peat cut from the distillery's own peat beds in the process, and this Hobbister Moor peat gives the finished whisky its characteristic heathery nose and flavour.

Orkney's second distillery, Scapa, 1990s. Scapa dates from 1885, and was saved from fire by naval ratings billeted there during the Second World War. During the same conflict, Canadian troops used the distillery's larch washbacks as baths! The 'make' of Scapa is a component of Allied Distillers' Ballantine's blend, and is less well known as a single malt than it deserves to be. Until 1928, Orkney could boast a third distillery, known as Man O'Hoy, which operated on a small scale in the centre of the port of Stromness.

Talisker distillery, Carbost, Isle of Skye, prior to a reconstruction programme undertaken during the early 1960s. Like many of the island distilleries, Talisker enjoys a magnificent location, standing on the shores of Loch Harport, and it was founded in 1830. The distillery was extended during the 1880s and again in 1900, though much of the present plant dates from the 1960s, and was built following a fire in the stillhouse. The powerful, peppery malt produced by United Distillers & Vintners at Talisker is a component of their heavily promoted 'Classic Malts' range.

Tobermory distillery, Isle of Mull, late nineteenth century. The distillery has its origins in the late eighteenth century, and after a chequered past and many periods of silence it is currently owned by Burn Stewart Distillers. Sadly for the character of the whisky, it is no longer matured in its island home, where it gained a maritime tang from its seaside location. As the distillery warehouses were sold for conversion into holiday apartments some years ago, the whisky is now shipped to Burn Stewart's Deanston distillery at Doune in Perthshire for maturation.

Isle of Jura distillery, from Small Isles Bay, undated. The island of Jura lies just a narrow stretch of water away from the isle of Islay, but the malt distilled on Jura shares none of the peaty, medicinal characteristics for which its neighbouring distilleries are famous. This is because the distillery uses only lightly peated malt, and is equipped with tall, high-necked stills. The original Jura distillery was founded in the island's tiny 'capital' of Craighouse during the early years of the nineteenth century, but the present complex dates from the early 1960s. It is now owned by JBB Brands (Greater Europe) plc.

Isle of Arran distillery, Lochranza, 1996. The Isle of Arran is Scotland's newest distillery, having opened in 1995. Prior to its construction, the last legal whisky-making operation on the island was at Lagg, and that closed in 1837. The Isle of Arran distillery is quite traditional in design, and incorporates impressive visitor facilities. Although still young, the single malt from the distillery is already shaping up to be something of a classic.

iv

ISLAY

Main Street, Bowmore, with the town's famous round church at the top of the hill, 1990s. Bowmore is the 'capital' of Islay, and home to the oldest of the island's seven working distilleries. Since the mid-eighteenth century, a total of twenty-three licensed distilleries have operated on Islay.

Bowmore distillery from Loch Indaal, 1990s. At high tide the seawater rises several feet up the side of the famous 'Warehouse No. 1 Vaults', and the maritime influences to which the maturing spirit is exposed help to shape its character. Bowmore distillery was founded in 1779, and stylistically it produces a smoky, slightly briny, medium-bodied whisky somewhere between the intense malts distilled on the southern shores and the lighter ones of the north. Bowmore still boasts its own operational floor maltings, and since 1994 has been owned by the Japanese company Suntory. Bowmore single malts have long enjoyed an enthusiastic following in Japan.

The Pibroch 'puffer' arriving at either Port Ellen or Ardbeg pier, late 1920s. In 1924, DCL purchased the Pibroch 'puffer' or coaster to service its Hebridean distilleries, and the vessel was a familiar sight around Islay and Skye until the advent of roll-on/roll-off ferries to Islay in 1974 brought to an end individual distillery deliveries by sea. The original coal-fired Pibroch was replaced during the late 1950s with a diesel-powered successor, which carried the same name.

Bruichladdich distillery, late nineteenth century. Bruichladdich began production on the western shore of Loch Indaal in 1881, a time when the growth in blended whisky sales created a great demand for malts. The new distillery was one of the first to be constructed from an innovative new building material called concrete. Bruichladdich is the most westerly distillery in Scotland and, following periods of silence, the plant's productive future was assured when it was purchased from JBB (Greater Europe) plc in late 2000 by a new firm called the Bruichladdich Distillery Company, headed by the independent whisky bottlers Murray McDavid.

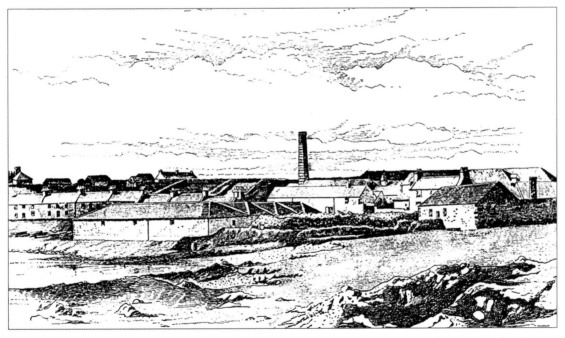

Lochindaal distillery, late nineteenth century. Lochindaal was situated at Port Charlotte, a couple of miles from Bruichladdich, and was built in 1829. A century after its opening, Lochindaal was acquired by DCL and taken out of production. The malt barns were subsequently incorporated into the Islay Creamery, while some warehouses continued to be used to mature whisky from other Islay distilleries for many years.

Port Ellen distillery, 1904. Port Ellen distillery was founded in 1825, and has an important place in the history of Scotch whisky. The spirit safe was developed there, and it was also at Port Ellen that Aeneas Coffey and Robert Stein conducted pioneering work on the patent still. The first direct export of whisky to the USA took place from Port Ellen distillery when it was owned by whisky magnate John Ramsay.

Port Ellen distillery and maltings, 1990s. Despite extensive modernisation in 1967, Port Ellen distillery was one of the DCL plants to close in 1983, and there seems little chance that whisky will ever be made there again, though the single malt is held in very high regard. The DCL maltings plant of 1973 dwarfs the distillery, and has the capacity to produce 400 tonnes of malted barley per week. It supplies a number of the island's distilleries.

Bessie Williamson working at the Laphroaig spirit safe, late 1950s. Laphroaig was established in 1815 by Alex and Donald Johnston, and the latter brother suffered the misfortune of dying in 1847 as the result of falling into a vat of pot ale. Laphroaig remained in the Johnston family until 1954, when, on the death of Ian Hunter, the distillery was bequeathed to Bessie Williamson, Hunter's company secretary. Laphroaig is now owned by Allied Distillers, and its pungent, peaty make has the distinction of being the only Islay malt to figure in the 'top ten' of world malt whisky sales.

Lagavulin distillery, with a vessel discharging its cargo at the pier, *c.* 1904. The rich, complex, smoky single malt of Lagavulin is the best-seller in UDV's 'Classic Malts' range, and an important constituent in many blends. The distillery traces its origins back to the 1740s, when no fewer than ten illicit stills were working close to Lagavulin Bay, though the present plant was founded in 1816. Once owned by the Mackie family of White Horse fame, Lagavulin subsequently passed to DCL, though today its make is still closely associated with the White Horse brand.

Ardbeg distillery from the sea, *c.* 1984. At the time, the distillery was in the ownership of Allied Distillers Ltd, whose principal focus was always on their neighbouring Laphroaig operation, and Ardbeg was functioning only on a care and maintenance basis. Note the scaffolding on the kiln pagoda in the centre of the picture.

Ardbeg's distillery manager Colin Elliot Hay, *c.* 1900. Current Ardbeg boss Stuart Thomson regretfully points out that today's managers do not live in quite such style! Since 1997, Ardbeg has been owned by Glenmorangie plc, which has invested heavily in the fabric of the site, and also in promoting Ardbeg single malt at a variety of ages. For many connoisseurs, Ardbeg is *the* Islay malt, managing to be very smoky and complex, yet at the same time quite delicate.

Colin Elliot Hay (left) and the staff of Ardbeg, *c.* 1902. Ardbeg was founded in 1815, making it the second-oldest surviving Islay distillery. Traditionally, Ardbeg used the most heavily peated malt in Scotland, operating its own floor maltings until the 1980s. Lack of fans in the malting house pagodas meant that instead of being drawn up quite rapidly, the peat smoke permeated very thoroughly through the malt, producing a distinctive pungency in the finished whisky. Ardbeg is currently purchasing heavily peated malt to ensure that future bottlings will retain the whisky's authentic character.

Bunnahabhain distillery, *c.* 1904. Like Bruichladdich, Bunnahabhain was established in 1881, and its name means 'mouth of the river' in Gaelic. Bunnahabhain is the most northerly distillery on Islay, and is situated in a remote, dramatic location. It was bought by Highland Distilleries Ltd in 1887, and is now a 'stablemate' of Highland Park and the Speyside trio of Glenrothes, The Macallan and Tamdhu. The capacity of Bunnahabhain was extended in 1963 from two to four stills, and the comparatively light-bodied single malt has been bottled since the 1970s. It enjoys extensive markets in France and the USA.

Caol Ila distillery, late nineteenth century. Caol Ila was established in 1846, and was in the ownership of Bulloch Lade & Co., at the time this engraving was made – note their name on the building to the right of the maltings. Bulloch Lade became the proprietors of Caol Ila in 1863, and were responsible for its extension in 1879. The distillery was taken over by DCL in 1927.

Caol Ila distillery, 1991. Along with Lagavulin and the Port Ellen site, Caol Ila is owned by UDV, whose predecessors DCL rebuilt the distillery in a strikingly modern style between 1971 and 1973, featuring their characteristic glass-fronted stillhouse (right) which enjoys spectacular views across the Sound of Islay to the neighbouring island of Jura. DCL increased Caol Ila's capacity from two to six stills during the 1970s reconstruction programme, making it one of the largest distilleries in the Hebrides.

v

CAMPBELTOWN

Kinloch distillery, wash, feints and spirit pumps, 1920s. Kinloch was one of Campbeltown's earlier distilleries, commencing production in 1823 on the site of a former maltings. Distilling ceased in 1926, and Kinloch's owner David MacCallum subsequently gave the distillery to the local authority as a site for housing.

Glen Scotia distillery, 1991. Scotia, as it was originally known, was founded in 1832, and in recent times the plant has experienced several periods of silence. Despite upgrading and modernisation carried out during the early 1980s – which saw its capacity extended from two stills to ten – Glen Scotia operated only intermittently during the last two decades of the twentieth century. It is currently owned by the Loch Lomond Distillery Co. Ltd, which began to undertake some distilling again during 2000.

Springbank distillery entrance, 1980s. Springbank is one of the few remaining family-owned distilleries in Scotland, and in the most traditional way imaginable it produces one of the world's great malts, complete with the characteristic saltiness associated with the Campbeltown style, which is not too far removed from some of the less assertive Islay malts. The distillery dates from 1828, and stands in Well Close, off Longrow, where it now incorporates parts of five defunct Campbeltown distilleries, namely Argyll, Longrow, Rieclachan, Springside and Union.

The former Benmore distillery, Saddell Street, 1991. Benmore was built in 1868 by Glasgow-based Bulloch Lade & Co, and in 1929 came into the ownership of DCL, though distilling had ceased two years earlier. Structurally, Benmore has survived better than most defunct Campbeltown distilleries, being sold to West Coast Motor Services by DCL, and operating as a bus depot ever since. The pagoda roof may have been removed from the former maltings, but Benmore was the first Campbeltown distillery to boast such a feature.

Lochhead distillery warehouses, Lochend Street, 1980s. Lochhead was founded in 1824, and from 1895 until 1920 it was owned by J.B. Sheriff & Co. Ltd, which expanded it at the turn of the century, though the operation already boasted the borough's biggest mash tun. Sheriff also had interests in Lochindaal and Bowmore distilleries on Islay, but when the company collapsed in 1920 Benmore Distilleries Ltd acquired Lochhead, which ultimately passed to DCL in 1929, a year after distilling had ceased. Much of Lochhead remained intact until the 1990s, when the site was cleared for a supermarket development.

The former Burnside distillery, latterly Campbeltown Creamery Ltd, 1991. Situated half a mile from the town centre in Witchburn Road, the creamery site was formerly home to Burnside distillery, which was operational between 1825 and the early 1920s. When the distillery closed, the premises were converted into a creamery, and the old buildings still stand at the heart of the expanded plant. The first reference to whisky-making in Kintyre dates from 1591, and a small-scale coal mine at Drumlemble, near Campbeltown, provided a comparatively cheap source of fuel for local distilleries until it closed in 1923.

The stillhouse, Hazelburn, late nineteenth century. Hazelburn distilled for exactly a century before succumbing to market forces in 1925, becoming Campbeltown's largest and most successful distillery along the way. In its heyday it boasted the ability to produce a quarter of a million gallons of whisky per year. Today the site of Hazelburn is a business park, incorporating some of the original buildings. In 1997 the Hazelburn name was revived by J. & A. Mitchell & Co. Ltd, owners of Springbank who applied it to a new triple-distilled Lowland-style single malt, due to be bottled for the first time in 2006.

vi

LOWLAND

Auchentoshan distillery, Duntocher, Dumbartonshire, 1990s.

Glenkinchie distillery staff, 1920s. Glenkinchie is situated near the village of Pencaitland, some 15 miles south-east of Edinburgh, and distilling began there in 1825. In 1914 it joined with fellow Lowland distilleries Rosebank, St Magdalene, Clydesdale and Grange to form Scottish Malt Distillers, which subsequently became a subsidiary of the Distillers' Company Ltd.

Glenkinchie distillery, 1990s. Glenkinchie remains licensed to UDV's John Haig & Co., and traditionally the malt was a major component of Haig blends. A ten-year-old Glenkinchie is UDV's regional representative in the 'Classic Malts' range, giving it the brightest future of any Lowland malt distillery. The whisky is light in body, aromatic and a nicely complex aperitif. In 1997 a new and highly impressive visitor centre opened at the distillery, complete with a fascinating 75-year-old scale model of the distillery.

Redundant still, Auchentoshan distillery, Duntocher, 1990s. Auchentoshan has belonged to Morrison Bowmore Distillers Ltd since 1984, and is the only surviving Scottish distillery that continues fully to triple-distil its spirit in a series of three stills. The practice was once common in Lowland distilleries, including at the now silent Littlemill plant at nearby Bowling. Triple-distillation allows the spirit to mature comparatively quickly, as well as producing a whisky that is light in character. Auchentoshan distillery was founded around 1800, and though classified as a 'Lowland', it draws its process water from a loch located north of the 'Highland Line'.

The stillhouse, Ladyburn distillery, Girvan, 1960s. Ladyburn was established by William Grant & Sons Ltd in 1966 within the company's large Girvan grain distillery, and made malt whisky for a decade. There was a trend, for a time, to produce malt whisky within predominantly grain distilleries, with Kinclaith emanating from the Strathclyde grain distillery in Glasgow, while Inverleven was made at the Dumbarton distillery. Examples of such whiskies are now extremely rare. Scotland's newest grain distillery, Loch Lomond at Alexandria, turns out a number of malts, including Inchmurrin and Old Rhosdhu.

The stillhouse, Bladnoch distillery, Wigtownshire, 1980s. Bladnoch is one of the few Lowland distilling stories with a happy ending, as this apparently 'lost' distillery was resurrected by Northern Irish entrepreneur Raymond Armstrong, and spirit began to flow again during 2001. Bladnoch is the most southerly distillery in Scotland, tucked away near the former Galloway county town of Wigtown, and it has produced one of the finest of all the Lowland drams.

Bladnoch stillman John Herries (left) and Raymond Armstrong, 2000. Bladnoch distillery was established around 1817 and operated until 1938, after which it remained silent for the next two decades. Bladnoch passed through various hands before being bought by Arthur Bell & Sons in 1983, subsequently becoming part of the United Distillers' empire. UD decommissioned the distillery in 1993, and Raymond Armstrong acquired it the following year, ultimately setting about restoring it to productive status. The initial intention is to distil small amounts of spirit to ensure supplies for the popular visitor centre shop.

Rosebank distillery, 1930s. Rosebank stands on the banks of the Forth–Clyde Canal, near Falkirk, and for many connoisseurs and industry experts it produced the true regional classic whisky. Rosebank is a well-balanced, elegant malt, quite dry and strongly scented. There was an element of surprise when United Distillers chose Glenkinchie for their 'Classic Malts' range, closing Rosebank in 1993. Given its more scenic location and its proximity to Edinburgh, however, Glenkinchie always had sounder claims as a visitor attraction than Rosebank, regardless of the merits of the two malts.

St Magdalene distillery, Linlithgow, 1999. Part of Linlithgow's redundant St Magdalene distillery has been developed for residential use, but retains its pagoda. Like Rosebank, St Magdalene stands close a canal, in this case the Union, and also has the advantage of being situated next to the main Edinburgh–Stirling railway line. The distillery was in production by 1797, and stands on the site of a twelfth-century leper hospital. St Magdalene was one of five distilleries to have operated in the historic West Lothian town, and from 1912 until closure in 1983 it was owned by DCL.

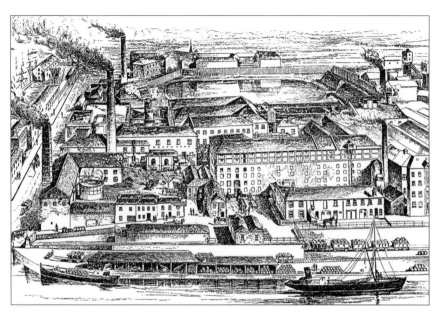

Dundashill distillery, Glasgow, late nineteenth century. Dundashill stood next to Port Dundas distillery, which has survived and is now one of UDV's two operational grain distilleries, while Dundashill has long since disappeared beneath a housing development. The distillery was founded around 1770, and grew to be a very large plant, covering 5 acres of ground and producing an average of 350,000 gallons per annum. Operated for many decades by the Harvey family, Dundashill closed in 1902, and was bought the following year by DCL, which used some of the buildings for storage and coopering, having dismantled the production equipment.

Grange distillery, Burntisland, Fife, late nineteenth century. Along with Grange, Fife had two other long-established distilleries at Auchtermuchty and Auchtertool, near Kirkcaldy. Grange began life in 1767 as a brewery, being converted to distilling some six years later. By the early twentieth century, Grange was a comparatively large-scale operation, turning out in excess of one-quarter of a million gallons of spirit per year, and boasting 19 warehouses for maturing spirit, not to mention its own gasworks. The distillery failed to survive the economic downturn of the 1920s, however, though some buildings and the 'listed' Georgian gates and high distillery wall remain intact.

Some Favourite Blends

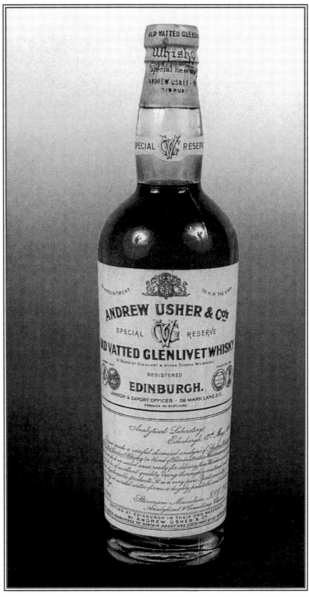

A bottling of Usher's Old Vatted Glenlivet, the forerunner of today's popular Scotch whisky blends.

THE BAILIE NICOL JARVIE

→ BLEND OF ←

Old Scotch Whisky,

PRODUCE OF
SCOTLAND

Sole Proprietors.

NICOL ANDERSON & Cº, LTP

QUEEN'S DOCK

LEITH

VERY OLD
RESERVE

Bailie Nicol Jarvie

This high-class blend is named after a Sir Walter Scott character who features in the novel *Rob Roy*, and the brand name was probably first used around 1860. The modern version is produced by Glenmorangie plc, which relaunched it in 1994, and 'BNJ' now enjoys a higher visibility than before. The black-on-white label remains unchanged by marketing-led initiatives, and the whisky itself has a very high (60 per cent) malt content, with the owning company's Glen Moray and Glenmorangie featuring strongly among the nine component malts. A beautifully balanced, complex whisky with quite a light yet mellow character.

Ballantine's Finest

One of numerous fine blends from the Allied Distillers' stable, Ballantine's is less well-known in Britain than it is in the rest of the world, where some five million cases are sold each year. European markets are particularly strong, though North American sales are also extremely impressive. The old company of George Ballantine & Son was acquired in 1937 by the Canadian distillers Hiram Walker, who proceeded to build Dumbarton distillery to supply the grain spirit requirements of their new purchase. Miltonduff and Glenburgie distilleries near Elgin were bought in order to provide malt. Finest is quite a soft, light-bodied blend, but has a distinctive tang of peat, and a comparatively complex profile.

Bell's

Blended whiskies produced by the Perth firm of Arthur Bell & Sons were selling all over the world in the late Victorian period, and by 1970 Bell's Finest was the market-leading blend in Scotland. A decade later it was the best-selling brand in the UK. In 1985, Bell's was purchased by Guinness, ultimately becoming part of UDV, and in 1994 the Bell's 'Extra Special' blend was relaunched as an eight-year-old, complete with a £15 million promotional campaign. The eight-year-old expression is well-balanced and slightly smoky, and contains some high-class Speyside malts, along with a little Caol Ila from Islay to add depth.

Black & White

The 'Buchanan Blend' was registered in 1880 by Canadian-born James Buchanan. Buchanan supplied his whisky to most of London's music halls, and also gained a lucrative contract to provide whisky for the House of Commons. The bottle was dark, with a very white label, and when people persisted in asking for 'black and white' whisky, Buchanan changed the name in 1905 to Black & White, adding the distinctive pair of contrasting terriers to the label at the same time. Today, as part of UDV, Black & White contains malts such as Dalwhinnie and the more robust Clynelish, although the character of today's brand is comparatively light and uncomplicated, with notes of heather and toffee on the nose and in the flavour.

Black Bottle
The Black Bottle brand name was first registered in 1879 by the Aberdeen company of Gordon Graham and Charles David – later Gordon Graham & Co, and long before it became better known, Black Bottle was popular with discriminating drinkers, particularly in its north-east homeland. In 1995, Black Bottle was acquired by Highland Distillers plc from Allied, and is now promoted as the blend 'with a Heart of Islay'. It contains malt from seven Islay distilleries, and is full-bodied, distinctly peaty, slightly salty, and with characteristic Islay iodine notes.

Chivas Regal
By the time that the Canadian distillers Seagram bought Chivas Bros in 1949, Chivas Regal was already one of the most successful Scotch whisky blends in North America, and it currently sells in more than 150 countries, being the world's leading premium brand. At the heart of this deluxe blend is the Speyside Strathisla malt, and as all of the distilleries built or acquired by Seagram are located on Speyside it comes as no surprise to find that Chivas Regal with its 40 per cent malt content boasts the delicate characteristics common to many Speyside malts, with fruit and spice on the nose and palate, and an overall sensation of sophistication.

Claymore

The Claymore name was first used during the 1890s, passing to DCL in 1925. Half a century later, the company decided to relaunch the brand as a lower-priced blend, and it subsequently became very popular in the UK market. In the wake of the Guinness takeover of DCL, Claymore was acquired by Whyte & Mackay, whose master blender Richard Paterson set about upgrading the blend, giving it far more body by using a higher proportion of older malts. Claymore remains something of a bargain-basement whisky, but this sweet, well-rounded blend now represents excellent value.

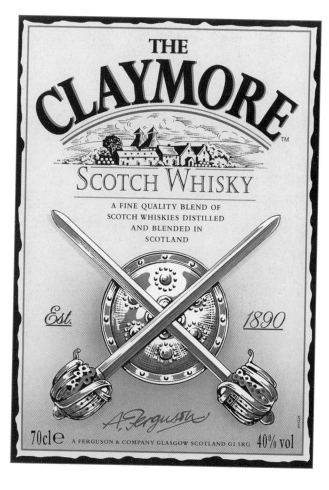

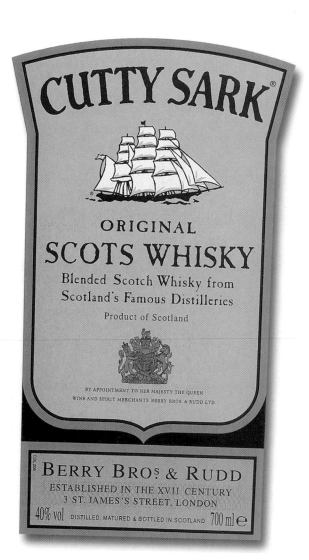

Cutty Sark

Developed in 1923 by leading independent wine and spirits merchant Berry Bros & Rudd Ltd, Cutty Sark was named after the famous clipper ship, which in turn took its name from Robert Burns' poem 'Tam O'Shanter'. Cutty Sark was the first light-coloured blend, smooth and crisp in character, and specifically designed to appeal to the American palate. In the years following the repeal of Prohibition (1933), Cutty Sark became one of the foremost blended Scotch whiskies in the USA, a position it still holds today. Cutty Sark contains some twenty malt whiskies, mostly from Speyside, and has a particularly strong following among younger drinkers in France, Greece, and Spain.

Dewar's White Label

White Label was developed in Perth by John and Tommy Dewar in the late nineteenth century, and is now the best-selling blended Scotch in the USA, and in the top five worldwide. Malt whisky produced at Dewars' Aberfeldy distillery in Perthshire has long been at the heart of White Label, which is a medium-bodied, sweet and slightly spicy blend today, whereas it was once much more robust. Its present character makes it ideally suited to export markets, and the brand sells in some 140 countries, with important markets in Greece and Spain, as well as the USA.

The Famous Grouse

Like Bell's and Dewar's, another enduring blended whisky to come out of Perth. The Famous Grouse was first developed during 1897 as the Grouse Brand by the firm of Matthew Gloag & Son, and its success soon led to the whisky being rebranded as The Famous Grouse. Since 1970, Gloag has belonged to Highland Distillers plc, and 'Grouse' is now the leading blend in the Scottish market, and the second-best seller in the UK. Inevitably, Highland Distillers' malts such as Tamdhu, Glenrothes and The Macallan feature in The Famous Grouse recipe, and the finished whisky is a most accomplished, well-rounded, quite light-bodied drink.

Grant's Family Reserve
William Grant & Sons Ltd's blend was developed during the late 1890s and was named Standfast after the Grant clan war-cry – 'Stand fast Craigellachie!' It is now marketed as Family Reserve, and is one of the fastest-growing blends in the world. It has a distinctive taste of Speyside about it, which is not surprising as Grant's Balvenie and Kininvie malts take pride of place, along with a dash of Glenfiddich. However, the blend also gains more robust, slightly smoky characteristics from the inclusion of Bowmore and Laphroaig from Islay.

Haig Gold Label
The famous company of John Haig & Co. began selling blended whiskies during the 1860s, and Gold Label – with its slogan 'Don't be vague, ask for Haig' – was the best-selling whisky in the UK by the time of the Second World War. The Lowland distillery of Glenkinchie remains licensed to John Haig & Co., and its malt is an important part of this UDV blend, along with the likes of the great and often underrated Speyside Linkwood. Gold Label has quite a high malt content which informs the character of this sweet, oaky blend.

119

Highland Queen
Along with Bailie Nicol Jarvie, Highland Queen is one of Glenmorangie plc's leading blends, and is named after Mary, Queen of Scots, who arrived from France at the port of Leith, aged eighteen, to take the Scottish crown in 1561. The offices of the blend's founders, MacDonald & Muir Ltd, were close to the spot where Mary Stewart disembarked. The present Highland Queen blend is much lighter and less robust than was formerly the case, but this is a very drinkable dram, with the owners' Glen Moray malt from Elgin featuring prominently in its make-up.

Isle of Skye
The Isle of Skye blend was created on its native island around a century ago by Ian MacLeod, and is now owned by Peter J. Russell & Co., an old-established whisky broking and blending company based in Broxburn, near Edinburgh. The eight-year-old version of Isle of Skye has a 40 per cent malt content, and Lagavulin and Talisker tend to dominate among the constituent malts. This is a peaty, smoky, full-bodied old-fashioned blend.

J&B Rare

The firm of Justerini & Brooks dates back to 1749, when one Giacomo Justerini arrived in London from Italy in (ultimately unsuccessful) pursuit of an opera singer. He proved more successful in the wine and spirits trade, however, and the company he helped to found formulated J&B Rare during the early 1930s specifically to appeal to the US market. Now part of the UDV empire, J&B is one of the leading blended Scotch brands in the USA, and the second best-selling blend in the world. J&B Rare is quite light, as one would expect of a blend popular in the USA, but delicate and sophisticated.

Johnnie Walker Black Label

The Johnnie Walker name was patented in 1908, and the 'Red Label' and 'Black Label' versions that are still so popular date from that time. Black Label is a deluxe expression, and gives Chivas Regal a serious run for its money as the leading deluxe whisky in export markets. In the ownership of UDV, the blenders of Black Label can draw on a very wide range of high-class, mature malts, and traditionally quantities of Cardhu and Craigellachie from Speyside, Aberfeldy from Perthshire and Caol Ila from Islay have helped to shape this elegant, complex example of the blenders' art. Black Label is rich and peaty, yet with a definite sweetness and notes of spice.

Johnnie Walker Red Label
Today, Johnnie Walker Red Label is the world's best-selling whisky, with just short of 8 million cases being sold during 1997. One hundred and twenty million bottles of the various Johnnie Walker blends are sold each year, with a dram being consumed somewhere every six seconds! Red Label is a full-bodied, quite traditional blend, with Talisker and Caol Ila giving a hint of the islands alongside quieter Speysides.

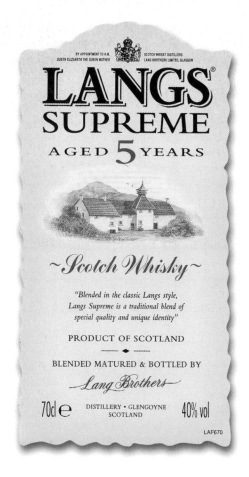

Langs Supreme
Langs Supreme is a rich, fruity, full-flavoured blend with a high percentage of malt to grain, and it is marketed as being aged for five years. Some twenty-five whiskies make up the blend, which is allowed to 'marry' in casks for nine months prior to bottling. The Glaswegian brothers Alexander and Gavin Lang set up as whisky blenders and merchants in 1861, being prosperous enough to purchase Glengoyne distillery fifteen years later. The comparatively light-bodied, unpeated single malt of Glengoyne lies at the heart of Lang's Supreme, which is owned by the Edrington Group.

Stewarts Cream of the Barley
Cream of the Barley is an Allied Distillers' blend, which has its roots in Alexander Stewart & Son's Dundee blending company. At the heart of the blend is malt whisky from the recently closed Glencadam distillery in the ancient Angus city of Brechin, though a total of some fifty malts are included. Cream of the Barley sells widely in supermarkets and off-licences at a competitive price, and is one of the best-selling Scotch whisky brands in Ireland.

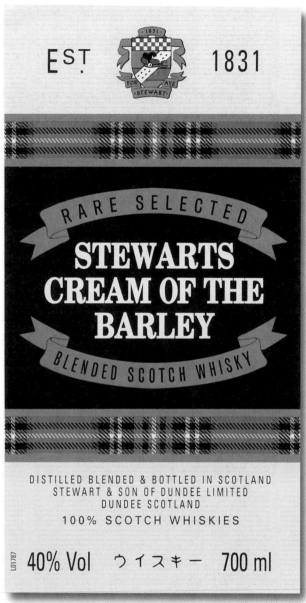

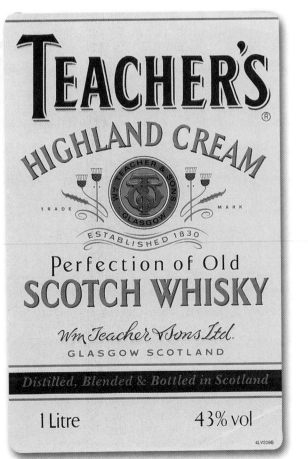

Teacher's Highland Cream
The firm of William Teacher & Son first registered the Highland Cream name in 1884, and today the brand is a mainstay of the Allied Distillers' stable, along with Ballantine's. Teacher's is the third-largest selling blend in the UK market and is in the 'top twenty' worldwide. Highland Cream contains at least 45 per cent malt, which is higher than many blends, and the fact that two of its principal constituent malts are the smoky, old-fashioned, much underrated Speysider Ardmore and the equally characterful nearby Glendronach, means that this is a delightfully full-bodied, rich and powerful whisky.

White Horse

White Horse whisky was named after a famous Edinburgh coaching inn on the Canongate that was for many years owned by the Mackie family, and the powerful malt from the same family's Lagavulin distillery on Islay lay at the heart of this distinctive blend. The White Horse brand name was registered in 1890, when Peter Mackie was controlling White Horse Distillers. Today's UDV-owned White Horse blend remains faithful to its Islay traditions, but the intensity of Lagavulin is backed up by the likes of such heavy-duty malts as Talisker and Clynelish, to give a distinctive, smoky, full-bodied blend.

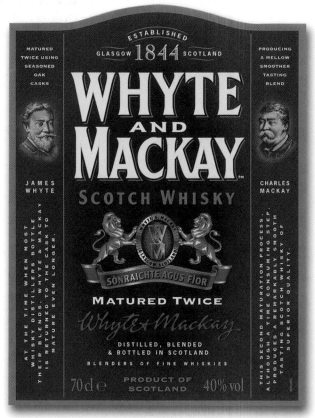

Whyte & Mackay

Whyte & Mackay's Special Blend was developed in Glasgow during the 1880s by James Whyte and Charles Mackay, and is notable for the fact that the component malts and grains are vatted separately for several months before being mixed together and allowed a further four months to 'marry' in the cask prior to bottling. Whyte & Mackay does well in export markets and has a loyal UK following. It is a well-rounded, malty, quite sweet whisky, with no particular dominant malt style, no doubt due to the rare process of marrying which the thirty-five or so constituent malts undergo.

Acknowledgements & Picture Credits

I owe a great debt of gratitude to many people who have given of their time and knowledge in support of this project. They include members of staff at numerous companies within the Scotch whisky industry, and also Simon Fletcher and Michelle Tilling at Sutton Publishing Ltd.

Special thanks are due to Bill Bergius of Allied Distillers Ltd, Fiona Buchanan of Glenmorangie plc, Peter Gordon of William Grant & Sons Distillers Ltd, Alan Greig of Chivas Brothers, Caroline Jones of United Distillers & Vintners Archive, Richard Joynson of Loch Fyne Whiskies, Inveraray, Rebecca Laurance of Cutty Sark International, Tommy Leigh of North British Distillery Ltd, Aoife Martin of United Distillers & Vintners Archive, Jaki Martin of Highland Distillers plc, Fiona Murdoch of the Whisky Shop, Dufftown, Richard Paterson of JBB (Greater Europe) plc, Avril Parkinson of the Edrington Group, Karen Prentice of the Scotch Whisky Association, David Robertson of The Macallan Distillers Ltd, Paul Robertson of Allied Distillers Ltd, Freda Ross of Highland Distillers plc, Iain Russell of the Heritage Works, Jacqui Sargeant of John Dewar & Sons Ltd, Yvonne Thackeray of Chivas Brothers, Stuart and Jackie Thomson of Ardbeg Distillery, Mary-Margaret Timpson of Inver House Distillers, and Jim Turle of the Edrington Group.

Photographs are reproduced by kind permission of the following:

Allied Distillers Ltd: pp. 7, 32 (upper), 53, 54, 90 (lower), 92 (lower), 99 (upper), 114 (lower), 116 (upper), 123; Chivas Brothers: pp. 8, 19 (lower), 21 (upper), 23 (lower), 26, 27, 33 (lower), 36 (lower), 51, 52, 60 (upper), 83, 84 (upper), 85, 86 (upper), 87, 88, 89, 116 (lower); Cutty Sark Scots Whisky: p. 117 (lower); John Dewar & Sons Ltd: pp. 20 (upper), 34 (upper), 40, 41, 42 (upper), 57 (lower), 73 (lower), 118 (upper); The Edrington Group: p. 75 (upper), 122 (lower); Jean Gillies: p. 63; Glenmorangie plc: pp. 22 (upper), 69 (upper), 77, 96 (lower), 100, 101 (upper); William Grant & Sons Distillers Ltd: pp. 12, 19 (upper), 21 (lower), 23 (upper), 32 (lower), 35, 36 (upper), 49, 50, 57 (upper), 78 (lower), 79, 80, 81 (upper), 109 (lower), 119 (upper); Highland Distillers plc: pp. 74, 82, 91, 92 (upper), 118 (lower); Inver House Distillers: pp. 15, 20 (lower), 67, 68 (lower), 84 (lower); Isle of Arran Distillers Ltd: p. 95 (lower); JBB (Greater Europe) plc: pp. 5, 10, 11, 25, 33 (upper), 55, 56 (upper), 60 (lower), 69 (lower), 76 (upper), 94 (upper), 117 (upper), 124 (lower); Bill Jones: p. 30 (lower); Margaret Kirkby: pp. 104, 105, 106 (upper); Loch Fyne Whiskies: p. 58 (upper); Morrison Bowmore Distillers Ltd: pp. 18 (lower), 95, 96 (upper), 109 (upper); Fiona Murdoch: p. 58 (lower); North British Distillery Ltd: pp. 28, 29, 30 (upper); Scotch Whisky Association: p. 62 (lower); Scotch Whisky Heritage Centre Ltd: p. 59 (upper); Speyside Cooperage Ltd: p. 24; United Distillers & Vintners Archive: pp. 31, 34 (lower), 37, 42 (lower), 43, 44, 45, 46, 47, 48 (upper), 71 (lower), 93 (upper), 98 (lower), 111 (upper), 115, 119 (lower), 121, 122 (upper), 124 (upper).